THE EVER-CHANGING UNION

AN INTRODUCTION TO THE HISTORY, INSTITUTIONS AND DECISION-MAKING PROCESSES OF THE EUROPEAN UNION

THE EVER-CHANGING UNION
AN INTRODUCTION TO THE HISTORY, INSTITUTIONS AND DECISION-MAKING PROCESSES OF THE EUROPEAN UNION

2ND REVISED EDITION

CHRISTIAN EGENHOFER
SEBASTIAN KURPAS
PIOTR MACIEJ KACZYŃSKI
AND LOUISE VAN SCHAIK

CENTRE FOR EUROPEAN POLICY STUDIES (CEPS)

BRUSSELS

The Centre for European Policy Studies (CEPS) is an independent policy research institute based in Brussels. Its mission is to produce sound analytical research leading to constructive solutions to the challenges facing Europe today. The views expressed in this publication are those of the authors writing in a personal capacity and do not necessarily reflect those of CEPS or any other institution with which the authors are associated.

The authors wish to express their appreciation to Daniel Gros, Keijen van Eijk, Michael Emerson, Jorge Núñez Ferrer and Paul Ivan.

Cover design: Jorge Núñez Ferrer

ISBN: 978-92-9079-980-1

Centre for European Policy Studies
Place du Congrès 1, B-1000 Brussels
Tel: 32 (0) 2 229.39.11 Fax: 32 (0) 2 219.41.51
e-mail: info@ceps.eu
Internet: www.ceps.eu

Contents

List of Figures

List of Tables

List of Boxes

Still an 'ever-changing Union'?

Authors' note: This fully revised second edition of the "The Ever-Changing Union" provides a concise overview of the EU's history as well as its institutional structures and decision-making processes as they stand following the entry into force of the Treaty of Lisbon.

The European Union and the Treaty of Lisbon

The entry into force of the Treaty of Lisbon on 1 December 2009 marked the end of a long and complicated process of comprehensive treaty revision that had commanded considerable political attention from both national governments and the European institutions. Tough negotiations, the rejection of the Constitutional Treaty by the electorates in two member states and the difficult ratification of the Treaty of Lisbon have taken their toll on the enthusiasm of national leaders for further treaty reforms.[1] Unlike past negotiations, no 'leftovers' were identified at the 2007 Intergovernmental Conference that would have to be dealt with in a future round of reforms. As such the Treaty of Lisbon is likely to be the last in a long series of treaties since the late 1980s[2] that have amended the existing treaties in a broad and general way.[3] Future treaty changes will probably be very limited in scope, like the change envisaged for the establishment of a European Stability Mechanism in response to the sovereign debt crisis in 2010.

---

[1] Austrian and British leaders have even committed to holding referenda for substantive future changes.

[2] Namely these are the Single European Act (1987), the Treaty of Maastricht (1993), the Treaty of Amsterdam (1999) and the Treaty of Nice (2003). The year indicates when the treaty entered into force.

[3] Legally speaking, the Lisbon Treaty amended the Treaty on European Union and the Treaty establishing the European Community.

If a treaty change only concerns certain policy-related parts of the EU Treaties and if it does not increase the competences already conferred to the EU by the Treaties, it can be adopted according to a new "simplified revision procedure", introduced by the Treaty of Lisbon.[4] Although major treaty changes thus seem very unlikely in the foreseeable future, this of course does not exclude – and may even enhance – initiatives for institutional reforms *within* or even *outside* the established treaty framework. The EU will thus continue to be an ever-changing Union, although in a different way and most likely at a slower pace than in the past 25 years, which have been marked by recurring, profound treaty changes.

The new Treaty in a nutshell: What is new?

The Treaty of Lisbon continues the tradition of changing the EU's institutional set-up without revolutionising it. It has maintained the Union's distinct *sui generis* character: the EU will carry on functioning in some policy areas (such as the internal market) with powers that are more centralised at the EU level (supranational decision-making) and in other policy areas (e.g. security and defence) as an international organisation, where states have veto powers and decisions are sometimes legally difficult to enforce (intergovernmental decision-making). The Treaty has increased the number of policy areas where supranational decision-making applies, following the 'Community method':[5] the European Commission makes a

---

[4] The revised Art. 48(6) TEU foresees a unanimous decision by the European Council and ratification by all member states according to their respective constitutional requirements, but neither a Convention nor an Intergovernmental Conference.

[5] With the Treaty of Lisbon the European Community ceased to exist and its legal successor became the European Union. However, it is appropriate to continue using the well-established expression 'Community method' as it is not a legal term. The Community method is used to describe the supranational mode of EU decision-making, as reflected in the 'ordinary legislative procedure' (formerly called 'co-decision procedure'). In a 2010 speech, German Chancellor Angela Merkel defined a new "Union method" by distinguishing it from the Community method, as "a combination of the community method and coordinated action by the member states" (speech by Federal Chancellor Angela Merkel at the Opening Ceremony of the 61st academic year of the College of Europe, Bruges, 2 November

legislative proposal that can then be amended by both the member states (represented in the Council of Ministers, or 'Council') and the European Parliament, generally on the basis of some sort of majority rule (qualified majority voting). The European Court of Justice normally has a full right of scrutiny over the legislative acts adopted. In other areas (mainly but not only foreign and security policy) the EU more often applies intergovernmental procedures, where member states are the dominant actors and decisions are taken unanimously. In all policy areas implementation is almost exclusively carried out by member states, although monitored to different degrees by the European Commission. In practice, as an overall result of the institutional set-up and the great number of actors and interests involved, a strong bias towards consensual decision-making is likely to persist in all policy areas.

The Treaty of Lisbon is intended to make the EU more democratic, efficient and transparent. In addition to general institutional innovations, existing policies have been revamped, some of them significantly. The most important changes relate to policies on external matters and those on the area of freedom, security and justice.

- To enhance democracy, the Treaty of Lisbon has given more powers to the democratically elected European Parliament and introduced an element of direct democracy with the European Citizens' Initiative. National parliaments, which risk losing power when action is deferred to the EU, have been given the right to monitor that the EU observes the principle of subsidiarity according to a special procedure.[6]

- Measures to improve the EU's efficiency include more policy areas being subject to qualified majority voting (instead of unanimity) and a full-time President of the European Council elected for two and a

---

2010   (http://www.bundeskanzlerin.de/Content/EN/Reden/2010/2010-11-02-merkel-bruegge.html)).

[6] The principle of subsidiarity stipulates that the EU should only act in those areas where the same result cannot be achieved just as well at the national or even at the regional or local levels. Typical examples where action at the European level would have 'added value' are on matters with cross-border externalities (e.g. environmental policies for cross-border pollution or EU-wide product standards to facilitate trade) or scale effects (e.g. joint research or joint external actions).

half years (instead of the six-monthly rotation of a national leader in the chair), just to give two examples.

• In terms of transparency, the Treaty states explicitly for the first time how competences are divided between the Union and the member states. It also strengthens the right of public access to documents, while the new provision for a withdrawal procedure highlights the fact that Union membership is voluntary with member states being free to leave.

In the area of freedom, security and justice, almost all decisions are now to be taken by qualified majority in the Council and not by consensus, as was partly the case in the past. The ordinary legislative procedure (previously called 'co-decision'), which gives the European Parliament the same power as the Council to amend legislative proposals from the European Commission, has been extended to the entire policy area. The change primarily concerns police cooperation and judicial cooperation on criminal matters (i.e. the former 'third pillar').[7]

From the beginning, one of the main motivations for the revision of the EU Treaties was the ambition to make the Union's foreign and external policies more effective and enhance its role on the international stage. As a consequence, the Treaty of Lisbon has merged the two positions of High Representative for Foreign Affairs and Security Policy in the Council and the Commissioner in charge of the external relations portfolio, who is now also *ex-officio* one of the vice presidents of the European Commission. This new 'double-hatted' position is supported by a new European diplomatic service, the European External Action Service, which is being set up at the time of writing. There are also further important changes in specific fields of the EU's external action, such as trade, development policy, and security and defence. These are presented in greater detail in chapter 11.

---

[7] After a transition period of five years, the European Court of Justice will also receive full judicial scrutiny over acts adopted on these matters (with the exception of the validity and proportionality of police operations and measures taken by the member states to maintain law and order or to safeguard internal security).

1. Introduction

The European Union is one of the world's economic superpowers. Yet it is not a state with an army and a police force employed to protect its people and property. Originally designed to end a cycle of devastating wars on the European continent, the EU has fulfilled this initial *raison d'être* by far. Today it is composed of 27 states (Figure 1) with 4 currently in the waiting room to join,[8] a population of over half a billion and an economy representing almost €12 trillion in GDP (Table 1). The story of the EU began over 50 years ago and it is set to remain a dynamic and flexible structure in the future – a 'work in progress' that has never been designed according to a master plan.

When analysing European integration a key aspect concerns the 'nature of the beast':[9] the EU is more than a regular international organisation, but less than a nation state. From the EU's early years onwards there has been heated debate on what the new European project should eventually look like. Some have called for a supranational European federation where member states would give up veto rights and transfer power to the European level. Others have favoured a more intergovernmental system, where member states would keep their veto and cooperate on a voluntary basis. In extreme terms, the two options pit a 'European federation' against a 'Europe of nation states'. The status quo with the Treaty of Lisbon in force continues to reflect the middle ground between the two preferences, often termed *sui generis*: the EU being a polity with its own, very special characteristics. In some respects, such as the supremacy of its law over national laws and its high stakes in policy-making for the internal

---

[8] Those waiting to join are Croatia, Iceland, the Former Yugoslav Republic of Macedonia (FYROM) and Turkey. Albania, Montenegro and Serbia have submitted their applications. Bosnia and Herzegovina as well as Kosovo are potential candidates.

[9] See H. Wallace, W. Wallace and M.A. Pollack, *Policy-Making in the European Union*, 5th edition, Oxford: Oxford University Press, 2005; see also A. Wiener and T. Diez, *European Integration Theory*, Oxford: Oxford University Press, 2004.

market, the EU possesses features similar to those of a federal state, while in other domains there is either no common EU policy or the rules of the Treaties only allow for a very thin layer of EU involvement. The EU also differs considerably from the classic federation such as that in the US or in Germany, because authority is not designated clearly in a hierarchical way, but rather dispersed among diverse levels of governance and among various institutions.

Figure 1. Map of the EU member states

Source: Authors' adaptation taken from http://www.presentationload.com.

Table 1. EU-27 – Key figures (selected statistics)

Population (1 January 2010)	501.1 million
Gross domestic product (GDP) (in 2010)	€12,284 billion
Average GDP per capita in PPS* (in 2009)	€23,600
Poorest member state, GDP per capita in PPS (2009)	Bulgaria: €9,676
Richest member state, GDP per capita in PPS (2009)	Luxembourg: €63,248
Number of official languages	23

* Purchasing power standard (PPS) measures the price of a comparable and representative basket of goods and services in each country.

Source: Eurostat (http://ec.europa.eu/eurostat).

2. Phases of EU development

The fundamental legal basis of the EU is a set of agreements among its member states: the EU Treaties. They are usually named after the place where they were signed. The negotiations among the EU member states on treaty revisions and amendments are known as Intergovernmental Conferences (IGCs).

Broadly speaking we can distinguish *four* phases of EU development (see Table 2).[10] The first stretches from the origins of the EU in the early 1950s to the demise of the Bretton Woods system in the early 1970s. The next period from the 1970s to the early 1990s initially saw a period of stagnation ('Eurosclerosis') followed by a reinvigoration of the European Community (EC) with the completion of the internal market (EC 1992). The third phase can be described as the post-Maastricht period, which finished with the adoption of the Treaty of Nice,[11] covering 1992–2000. After Nice, the EU entered a fourth phase, which was dominated by a debate on the relationship of an enlarging EU with the powers of the individual member states (i.e. on EU

---

[10] Although the creation of the European Union only came about with the Treaty of Maastricht (1993), the term is also used for the preceding period in this text for reasons of linguistic continuity.

[11] The Treaty of Nice entered into force in 2003.

competences), as well as with EU citizens (i.e. on support for the EU) and with non-EU countries (i.e. on the EU's external policy role). This debate led first to a Constitutional Treaty for the EU, which was agreed upon in June 2004. But the Treaty failed to be ratified by all EU member states, being voted down in referenda in France and the Netherlands. In the first half of 2007 agreement was reached on a text that took up most of the elements of the Constitutional Treaty. Unlike the Constitutional Treaty, however, the new text would *not replace* the existing Treaties, but returned to the traditional practice of *amending* them. It was signed by the EU's political leaders on 13 December 2007 in Lisbon, which also gave the text its name: the Treaty of Lisbon. Following ratification in all member states according to their respective national provisions, the Treaty entered into force on 1 December 2009. In the following year some important aspects still had to be implemented by way of legislative acts, such as the European External Action Service mentioned above or the European Citizens' Initiative, through which EU citizens will be able to ask (but not force) the European Commission to present new policy initiatives in its areas of competence.

Table 2. Phases of European integration

Phase	Period	Developments/events	Legal form & treaty base (as amended)
1	1950–70	From its origins to the end of the Bretton Woods system (1950–70)	ECSC, Euratom, EEC Treaty of Rome
2	1970–92	From Eurosclerosis to revitalisation through 'EC 1992'	EEC Single European Act, Treaty of Maastricht
3	1992–2001	Post-Maastricht and beyond: Monetary union and steps towards political union	EC & EU Treaty of Maastricht, Treaty of Amsterdam, Treaty of Nice (in force 2003)
4	2001–10	Post-Nice: Failure of the Constitutional Treaty; Treaty of Lisbon	EU Treaty of Lisbon

Source: Authors' compilation.

Phase 1 – From its origins to the end of the Bretton Woods system (1950–70)

The history of the EU begins with the European Coal and Steel Community (ECSC), which was founded in the early 1950s and based on the Schuman Plan. The underlying philosophy of the Schuman Plan, which created rules for a common steel, iron and coal market, was to withdraw French and German basic industries from national authority in order to make another war impossible. Six European states decided to cooperate to achieve this aim: Belgium, France, Germany, Italy, Luxembourg and the Netherlands. In political terms, the ECSC can be considered a success, not least because it was a first important step in the European integration process. Over the last two decades, its substantive provisions have been gradually submerged into the Treaty establishing the European Economic Community (see the discussion below), eventually leading to its expiry in 2002.[12]

In addition to the initiatives eventually leading to the EU, many other organisations that shaped the post-war era were founded, including NATO and the OECD (for an overview see appendix 1).

An early move towards political union was the attempt to create a European Defence Community. Discussed after the successful launch of the ECSC, the defence community foresaw the integration of the armies of the six ECSC member states (including Germany) into a European army. In the end the project failed because the French parliament (more specifically the Assemblée Nationale) refused to ratify the Treaty for fear of transferring sovereignty over national defence policy. This period (1952–53) also saw the abortive attempt to create a European Political Union, which sought an integrated European foreign policy.

Following these failures, efforts to bring forward European integration moved away from political and towards economic cooperation. The Treaties of Rome,[13] signed in 1957, successfully reinvigorated the dynamism of the integration process through economic integration. The European Economic Community was

---

[12] The ECSC expired in mid-2002 after 50 years of existence.

[13] The "Treaties" here refer to the Treaty on the European Economic Community and the Euratom Treaty.

founded to overcome the sectoral limitations of the ECSC. It aimed at developing a common market for all economic sectors through an intermediary step, the creation of a customs union. In practical terms internal quotas and border tariffs among member states were abolished and replaced by a common external tariff. These steps changed the business environment in Europe once and for all. The common external tariff also marked an important shift in international relations, since it implied that it was no longer possible for individual member states to conclude bilateral trade agreements in the areas covered by the EEC, an important aspect of external relations. A common commercial policy on trade was formulated, for which the High Authority (now the European Commission) was given the prerogative to represent the Community externally (usually on the basis of a mandate approved by the member states).

Atomic energy was another area in which the pooling of national sovereignty was envisaged. In 1957 one of the Treaties of Rome established the European Atomic Energy Community (Euratom) to bring atomic energy under the European umbrella. The reasons for intensified cooperation in this field were the fear of energy import dependence in the aftermath of the Suez crisis[14] and the wish to reduce dependence on US and Soviet military (and with it political) dominance. National governments stuck to their desire to control their national programmes, however, and the need for nuclear energy only became apparent again with the first oil shock in 1973, by which time Euratom had already lost some of its original standing.

An important driver of the European integration process during the 1960s and 1970s was the European Court of Justice (ECJ). With landmark rulings it confirmed the primacy of EU law over national law and established the direct application of EU law (i.e. not necessitating transposition by national authorities). Through its rulings the ECJ

---

[14] During the Suez crisis, the UK, France and Israel fought a war against Egypt at the end of October 1956, following Egypt's decision to nationalise the Suez canal. Although initially the three allies were largely successful, pressure from the US and the Soviet Union forced the allies to withdraw. The outcome of the Suez crisis is generally seen as a signal of the weakening of British and French global influence.

helped to make up for deadlock on the political scene, where some European leaders opposed deeper integration. French President Charles De Gaulle, for instance, tried to strip the High Authority of its supranational aspirations with an attempt to assert the primacy of member states. He also attacked majority voting in the Council of Ministers by boycotting Council meetings and paralysing EU decision-making for several months. This so-called 'empty-chair crisis' resulted in the 'Luxembourg compromise', according to which member states acknowledged a national veto for policies that are against the 'vital' interests of one country. As a consequence, actual voting in the Council of Ministers remained the exception and consensus the rule.

Internationally, this phase ended with the demise of the Bretton Woods system of fixed currency exchange rates in the 1970s.

Phase 2 – From Eurosclerosis to revitalisation through EC 1992

The collapse of the Bretton Woods system signalled the beginning of a period of slow growth and a general economic crisis. Member states resorted to national measures to protect their currencies and their industries. The results were non-tariff barriers to trade and an increasing economic divergence that threatened achievements such as the common market and the common agricultural policy. This period is usually referred to as 'Eurosclerosis'.

The European Commission reacted by pursuing an active competition policy while member states, after they realised that national solutions had only made matters worse, became more willing to deepen European integration. This gave rise to a new agenda built around three principle objectives: the European monetary system (EMS), the internal market and further coordination of foreign policy matters by the member states. The EMS was designed to stabilise the currencies and achieve price stability. The priority of price stability, promoted especially by Germany, gradually became accepted by the EU and member states. The internal market programme of the European Community ('EC 1992') was a move on the part of businesses and governments to foster the macroeconomic conditions at the European level for a healthy economy and, in particular, to enable European companies to compete successfully in international markets. Business leaders began to lobby the European Commission for a vast expansion of common EU rules to govern trade among the member states with respect to non-tariff barriers. This culminated in a treaty reform, the Single European Act (SEA), entering into force in 1987. The SEA aimed at establishing an internal market with the target date of 1992 for its completion.[15] In practical terms, over the period 1987–92 numerous legislative measures were introduced to remove non-tariff trade barriers and forge an internal market.

The development of a common foreign and security policy was more difficult and in the end marked by little progress during this period. The EU's external powers remained largely centred around its external trade relations, which it used to grant preferred access to the EU market for countries whose economic development it wanted to support, such as the former colonies. This was coupled with an emerging development cooperation policy, which was targeted at the former colonies as well, and assisted EU member states in neutralising their often-distressed relations with them.

During the second phase of development important enlargements took place. In 1973 the UK, Ireland and Denmark joined, as did Greece in 1981 and Portugal and Spain in 1986, with the latter three collectively referred to as the 'southern enlargement'. A major motive for the southern enlargement was to provide political stability for countries that had experienced a difficult transition from dictatorship to democracy. There were also a number of important institutional changes. First, as a reaction to the (oil) crisis of the 1970s and a rapidly changing international environment after the demise of the Bretton Woods system, European heads of state and government began to meet on a regular basis. In 1974, these meetings were formally established as the European Council, which over time began to provide political and strategic leadership to the EU. The regular European Council meetings (at that time, two to four per year) also increased the international visibility of the EU.[16] Second, from 1979 the European Parliament was directly elected and the SEA enhanced the role of the European Parliament in the decision-making process. Finally, qualified majority

---

[15] A. Cockfield, *The European Union: Creating the Single* Market, Chichester: John Wiley and Sons, 1994, makes interesting reading.

[16] This was also the time around which the G-7 was launched.

voting was extended to basically all areas related to the internal market. This move strengthened the EU's supranational coverage, as it increased the number of areas in which member states would not be able to block a decision with their veto.

Phase 3 – Post-Maastricht and beyond, with monetary union and steps towards political union

The third period reflected both internal and external factors giving a boost to the European project. Internally the success of the single market programme and the relative success of the EMS had provoked thought about a monetary union in which member states could share a common currency. Externally the collapse of the Soviet Union catapulted the EU into leadership, as German reunification raised concerns about a changing European power balance and Central and Eastern European countries (CEECs) looked towards EU membership. Transatlantic relations also contributed to favourable conditions for European integration, with the US demonstrating renewed interest in political cooperation at the European level under President George H.W. Bush.

As a first tangible outcome, the Maastricht Treaty was signed by the then 12 member states in 1992. The Treaty introduced new policy areas at the European level that greatly expanded the Union's agenda. It turned the European Economic Community into the European Community, illustrating the broadening scope for cooperation beyond purely economic issues. The Treaty was also a demonstration of the ambition to tackle the imbalance between an 'economic giant' and a 'political dwarf' that was often used to describe the European Community. The Treaty of Maastricht embodied a first attempt at a common approach in policy areas that had hitherto been considered the traditional competences of sovereign states. It introduced EU citizenship (which nevertheless remained dependent on citizenship of an EU member state), a structure for cross-border police cooperation (Europol), a common approach towards immigration policy and a common foreign and security policy (CFSP). In reaction to the wish of some member states to keep national control over foreign affairs as well as justice and home affairs, a pillar structure of three different pillars was established under a common EU roof.

The first pillar covered the activities of the old EC Treaties, i.e. the policy areas where the EU has strong competences and where the 'Community method'[17] applied (often with qualified majority voting – see chapter 4). In the other pillars, decision-making was organised according to the 'intergovernmental method' (with unanimity required), which applied to the common foreign and security policy (second pillar) and justice and home affairs (third pillar, see Figure 2). Parts of justice and home affairs were subsequently moved to the first pillar by the Treaty of Amsterdam (1999), as trust among member states and the pressure for cooperation (on visas, asylum and immigration) had grown. In the second and third pillars, member states retained their right to veto and the European Commission, the European Parliament and the European Court of Justice played only a (very) limited role.

The Maastricht Treaty also consolidated the institutional framework of the first pillar. It further enhanced the role of the European Parliament by introducing the co-decision procedure for a great number of policy areas, thus giving the Council of Ministers and the European Parliament equal standing when deciding upon legislation (see chapter 4).

Probably the most important achievement of the Maastricht Treaty, however, was the introduction of the euro as a common currency, which has been managed by the European Central Bank (ECB) since 1999. Membership in the Economic and Monetary Union (EMU) entails a major step for the participating states, as it includes giving up authority to control the level of interest rates and tying national public finances to the Stability and Growth Pact with rules for the national budget deficit. Before 1999, in some member states drastic reforms to economic policies were required to meet the criteria for participation. Three member states decided not to participate: the UK, Denmark and Sweden. All 'new' EU member states that joined in 2004 and 2007 are obliged to eventually become members of the EMU. Slovenia was the first to do so in January 2007, followed by Cyprus and Malta in 2008 and Slovakia in 2009. Estonia became the 17th member of the eurozone on 1 January 2011.

---

17 See footnote 5.

Figure 2. The EU pillar structure as established by the Treaty of Maastricht

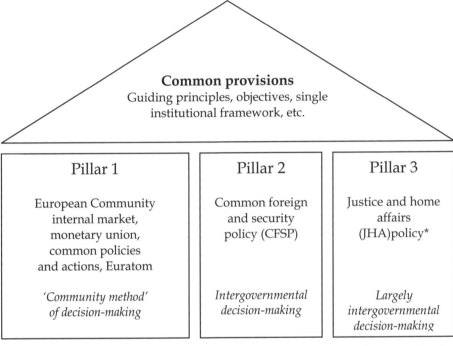

Common provisions
Guiding principles, objectives, single
institutional framework, etc.

Pillar 1	Pillar 2	Pillar 3
European Community internal market, monetary union, common policies and actions, Euratom	Common foreign and security policy (CFSP)	Justice and home affairs (JHA)policy*
'Community method' of decision-making	*Intergovernmental decision-making*	*Largely intergovernmental decision-making*

* Subsequently, under the Treaty of Amsterdam, this pillar was formally renamed police and judicial cooperation in criminal matters (PJCC).

Note: Before the Treaty of Lisbon made the European Union the legal successor of the European Community, both names were often used interchangeably. As Figure 2 illustrates, however, the European Community only covered the first pillar, as the most integrated part of the European Union. In essence the first pillar incorporated 'traditional EU business' like the single market, while the other two pillars covered 'new' policy areas. Pillars 2 and 3 remained largely intergovernmental.

Besides the deepening of integration, there was also a further widening of the Union: in 1995 Sweden, Austria and Finland joined the EU. The European Economic Area (EEA) Agreement was signed with Norway, Iceland and Liechtenstein. In practice, under the EEA Agreement these three countries implement the vast majority of internal market legislation although they do not take part in the EU's decision-making structures and the definition of the Union's political objectives (see appendix 1). A series of bilateral sector agreements containing similar arrangements were concluded with Switzerland. In addition, it was agreed that both Switzerland and Norway pay contributions for social and economic cohesion in the enlarged EU.[18]

The Treaty of Maastricht was followed by the Treaty of Amsterdam in 1997. This treaty revision dealt with the unfinished business left over from Maastricht, such as streamlining decision-making, increasing transparency and other institutional aspects. Specific achievements were new Treaty provisions on the so-called 'enhanced cooperation' procedure. This instrument allows a number of member states to initiate or move on with a common policy, while others do not participate. Under normal circumstances the EU moves at the pace of the slowest, leaving considerable leeway for individual states to block policies. At the same time there has always been the concern that too much flexibility ('Europe-à-la-carte') may risk undermining the coherence of the Union. The provisions on enhanced cooperation try to balance these two aspects and allow for flexible integration *within* the Treaty framework. Until very recently, however, such initiatives have only been taken *outside* the EU Treaties.[19] The best-known example is the Schengen Agreement of 1985, which abolished border (e.g. passport) controls. It was initially signed by just five of the then ten member states.[20] Subsequently almost all EU member states have become parties to the Schengen Agreement, and the Agreement has been integrated into the institutional and legal framework of the EU.[21] The acceptance by all member states of introducing the enhanced cooperation clause into the Treaties also stemmed from the understanding that if flexibility *within* the Treaties is not possible, it will most likely be exercised outside

---

[18] For further information, see the External Relations website of the European Commission on the countries in the European Free Trade Association (http://ec.europa.eu/external_relations/eea/country.htm).

[19] On 24 March 2010 the European Commission adopted its first proposal for a Council Decision authorising enhanced cooperation, more specifically its *Proposal for a Council Decision authorising enhanced cooperation in the area of the law applicable to divorce and legal separation* (COM(2010) 104 final/2, Brussels).

[20] At that time they were still operating in the context of the EEC.

[21] Even non-EU members Norway and Iceland have become members of the Schengen area, while the UK and Ireland along with Romania, Bulgaria and Cyprus remain outside (e.g. passport controls apply).

the EU framework anyway, but will leave the non-participating member states outside with even less influence.

The Treaty of Amsterdam also established an 'area of freedom, security and justice' in the EU, which includes external border controls, visa, asylum and immigration policy and judicial cooperation. After a period of trust-building, member states were ready to move these policies (with some restrictions) from the intergovernmental third pillar to the supranational first pillar. The same Treaty also brought improvements to the efficiency and effectiveness of the common foreign and security policy. A key innovation was the establishment of the High Representative for the CFSP. From 1999 to 2009 this position was held by Javier Solana, whose task was to assist the rotating presidency of the EU in taking care of the external representation of the EU on CFSP matters.

While the Treaty of Amsterdam introduced safeguards against governments in "serious and persistent" breach of the Union principles (Art. 7 TEU), it failed to address a number of key institutional issues, which became known as the 'Amsterdam leftovers':

- the size and composition of the European Commission,
- the weighting of votes in the Council (i.e. the voting shares of the individual member states), and
- possible extension of qualified majority voting in the Council.

At its Cologne summit in June 1999 the European Council decided to convene a new Intergovernmental Conference and resolve these issues before the end of 2000 in order to allow for the Union's Eastern enlargement.

Phase 4 – Post-Nice and the long process towards a new EU Treaty

At the Intergovernmental Conference in Nice, the core agenda consisted of the three Amsterdam leftovers outlined above (for instance, on the voting shares in the Council, see Table 3), notably to make the EU fit for enlargement. Agreement, culminating in the Treaty of Nice, was found after very difficult negotiations and with a result that was generally perceived as the lowest common denominator.

Table 3. *Seats in the European Parliament and votes in the Council of Ministers according to the Nice Treaty*

Country	Seats in the European Parliament*	Votes in the Council**	Population in 2010 (in millions)
Germany	99	29	81.8
France	72	29	64.7
UK	72	29	62.0
Italy	72	29	60.3
Spain	50	27	46.0
Poland	50	27	38.2
Romania	33	14	21.5
Netherlands	25	13	16.6
Greece	22	12	11.3
Belgium	22	12	10.8
Portugal	22	12	10.6
Czech Republic	22	12	10.5
Hungary	22	12	10.0
Sweden	18	10	9.3
Austria	17	10	8.4
Bulgaria	17	10	7.6
Denmark	13	7	5.5
Slovakia	13	7	5.4
Finland	13	7	5.3
Ireland	12	7	4.5
Lithuania	12	7	3.3
Latvia	8	4	2.2
Slovenia	7	4	2.0
Estonia	6	4	1.3

Table 3. cont'd

Cyprus	6	4	0.8
Luxembourg	6	4	0.5
Malta	5	3	0.4
Total	**736**	**345**	**501.1**

* Figures represent the number of Members of the European Parliament (MEPs) after the 2009 European elections that still took place on the basis of the Treaty of Nice. The total number of seats in the European Parliament was temporarily higher (785) than the 736 foreseen by the Treaty due to Romanian and Bulgarian deputies having joined mid-term in January 2007. With the Treaty of Lisbon the maximum number of MEPs is set at 751. Germany has lost 3 seats, while Spain has gained 4 seats, Austria, France and Sweden each have gained 2 seats and Bulgaria, Italy, Latvia, Malta, the Netherlands, Poland, Slovenia and the UK have each gained 1 seat. At the time of writing, ratification of a small treaty change was underway to make it possible for the additional MEPs to take office during the 2009–14 legislature, while all 99 German MEPs will serve the full five-year term until 2014.

** Qualified majority: for adoption, a proposal must be backed by

• 255 votes from a total of 345 (about 73.9% of the votes);

• plus a majority of member states (or two-thirds in certain cases).

Furthermore, any member state may request the verification that countries supporting the proposal represent at least 62% of the total EU population.

From 2014 onwards the new Lisbon rules for QMV will apply. These entail that a majority is obtained if

• 55% of the EU member states support the proposal,

• which represents at least 65% of the EU population;

nonetheless, until 2017 a request can be made to use the old rules.

Source: Authors' compilation.

The Treaty of Nice also extended the application of the enhanced cooperation mechanism to the area of CFSP, while matters with military or defence implications remained excluded.[22] The new Treaty abolished

---

[22] The Treaty of Lisbon has nevertheless introduced a new mechanism for flexible integration in the field of defence: permanent structured cooperation (Arts. 42(6) and 46 TEU as well as Protocol No. 10). To take part in permanent structured cooperation on defence, member states must meet certain criteria regarding their military capabilities, assessed in cooperation with the European Defence Agency (Art. 3 of Protocol No. 10 on Permanent Structured Cooperation). The agency – dealing with defence capabilities' development,

the possibility of any one country blocking an initiative and it reduced the number of countries necessary to embark on enhanced cooperation from a majority to the fixed number of eight.[23] Even so, an initiative can only go ahead if non-participants are not adversely affected by the cooperation and if they have the possibility to join at a later stage. The Treaty of Nice only entered into force in February 2003 after a second referendum in Ireland, which reversed an initial rejection.

Many thought that the innovations of the Treaty of Nice were insufficient to prepare the EU for enlargement along with other challenges, such as a perceived 'democratic deficit' of the EU. As a consequence, as early as December 2001 European heads of state met at a summit in Laeken (Belgium) and decided to convene a Convention on the Future of Europe to prepare a more profound revision of the Treaties. It ultimately resulted in a text seeking a complete overhaul of the institutional framework, in the form of a draft Constitutional Treaty.

Whereas in the past treaty changes were solely decided by government representatives behind closed doors in Intergovernmental Conferences, the Convention embodied a new model. Chaired by former French President Valery Giscard d'Estaing, it was not only composed of government representatives, but also national and EU parliamentarians and the European Commission. Furthermore, besides nationals from member states, the Convention included representatives from the then candidate countries.[24] The assembly managed to agree on a draft Constitutional Treaty that formed the starting point and blueprint for subsequent negotiations among EU member states in the Intergovernmental Conference. In June 2004, under the Irish EU presidency agreement was eventually reached. A month earlier, in May 2004, the EU had also enlarged and accepted ten new member states

---

research, acquisition and armament – has also been formally included in the EU Treaties (Art. 42(3) TEU and Art. 46 TEU).

[23] The Treaty of Lisbon has increased this number to nine.

[24] For more information on the Convention, see K. Kiljunen, *The European Constitution in the Making*, Centre for European Policy Studies, Brussels, 2004; P. Norman, *The Accidental Constitution*, 2nd edition, EuroComment, Brussels, 2005; and P. Ludlow, *The Making of the New Europe*, EuroComment, Brussels, 2004.

(Cyprus, the Czech Republic, Estonia, Hungary, Latvia, Lithuania, Malta, Poland, Slovakia and Slovenia), constituting the EU's biggest enlargement. In January 2007, the EU finalised the enlargement round, for which preparations had begun in the late 1990s, with Bulgaria and Romania also becoming members.

As with all reforms to the EU Treaties, the entry into force of the Constitutional Treaty necessitated ratification by all EU member states – either by their respective national parliaments or through referenda. Eighteen countries approved the Treaty, of which two (Spain and Luxembourg) did so through referenda. Nevertheless, the Constitutional Treaty never entered into force after referenda in France and the Netherlands returned negative results in May and June 2005. The reasons for the 'no' votes were multiple and ranged from unrelated issues like dissatisfaction with ruling national governments to Euroscepticism and lack of information about the text (particularly in the Netherlands) or a general perception of the EU as being too economically liberal and not 'social' enough (particularly in France).[25]

After what was termed a 'period of reflection', the treaty reform process was put back on track during the German EU presidency in the first of half of 2007. At the European Council in May 2007 European leaders agreed on a detailed mandate for another Intergovernmental Conference. This IGC agreed on a text that preserved most of the content of the Constitutional Treaty, but stripped the text of its constitutional symbolism. Instead of replacing the existing Treaties, the new Treaty would again amend them – as the Treaty of Amsterdam and the Treaty of Nice had done so before. With more protocols, declarations and safeguard clauses, the new Treaty of Lisbon added another layer to the existing ones, thereby not making any simpler the

---

[25] See European Commission, *The European Constitution: Post-referendum survey in the Netherlands*, Flash Eurobarometer 172, Brussels, June 2005 (http://ec.europa.eu/public_opinion/flash/fl172_en.pdf); see also European Commission, *La Constitution européenne: sondage post-référendum en France*, Flash Eurobarometer 171, Brussels, June 2005 (http://ec.europa.eu/public_opinion/flash/fl171_fr.pdf).

structure of the existing Treaties (renamed the Treaty on European Union (TEU) and the Treaty on the Functioning of the European Union (TFEU)).

Starting immediately after heads of state and government signed the Treaty in Lisbon on 13 December 2007, the ratification process took almost two years and faced a number of challenges. In Ireland, the first referendum on 12 June 2008 resulted in rejection. At the European summit in December 2008 the Irish government indicated its willingness to hold a second referendum on the Treaty in 2009. In return national leaders agreed that Ireland would be provided legal assurances that the Treaty of Lisbon would not grant the EU any additional powers on a number of issues identified as sensitive by the Irish government (taxation, the right to life, education and family, and security and defence) and also that there would continue to be one Commissioner per member state beyond 2014. After these guarantees were given, a second successful referendum was held on 2 October 2009.[26]In the summer of the same year, the Federal Constitutional Court of Germany gave a ruling on the legality of the new treaty with the German Constitution[27] allowing the President to conclude the German ratification. After the second Irish referendum, the Polish and the Czech

---

[26] The legal guarantees have taken the initial form of a decision by the heads of state and government, which is legally binding and which entered into force at the same time as the Treaty of Lisbon. In the future, the legal guarantees will then take the form of a protocol that will be attached to the EU Treaties. In the same context, the heads of state and government also agreed on a "Solemn Declaration on Workers' Rights and Social Policy", confirming the high degree of importance the Union attaches to these issues. The European Council of December 2008 also agreed that a decision would be taken to the effect that the European Commission shall continue to include one national of each member state beyond 2014.

[27] The Court found the Treaty of Lisbon to be compatible with the German Constitution, but demanded changes to the German ratification law. It was revised to strengthen the position of the German parliament (Bundestag and Bundesrat) concerning government action at the EU level. The text of the judgment of 30 June 2009 is available in English on the website of the Bundesverfassungsgericht (http://www.bundesverfassungsgericht.de/entsch eidungen/es20090630_2bve000208en.html).

Presidents[28] also signed their respective ratification instruments, and the Treaty of Lisbon entered into force on 1 December 2009.

With the Treaty of Lisbon, the EU attained a single legal personality and became the legal successor of the European Community. As a consequence the pillar structure established by the Treaty of Maastricht was abolished. Yet one policy area, CFSP, largely continues to follow intergovernmental rules, with the Lisbon Treaty even explicitly stating that CFSP "is subject to specific rules and procedures".[29] In this area, the adoption of EU legislative acts remains excluded. In contrast, with very few exceptions, matters that came under the former third pillar on justice and home affairs were brought under the co-decision procedure, now referred to as the 'ordinary legislative procedure'.[30]

To understand the EU, it is important to bear in mind that it remains a work in progress. While national leaders have little interest in major treaty changes that would create new competences or authority for the EU, and as a consequence require referenda in a number of member states, the Treaty of Lisbon allows for limited treaty changes in the "simplified revision procedure".[31] Such changes may not increase EU competences and are limited to Part III of the TFEU, which covers essentially all EU internal policies, such as those on the internal market,

---

[28] To meet the concerns of the Czech President Vaclav Klaus, the European Council agreed on a draft protocol providing for the extension of Protocol No. 30 to the Czech Republic, thus providing the same clarifications on the application of the Charter of Fundamental Rights of the EU in the Czech Republic as for the UK and Poland. Similar to the Irish legal guarantees, this agreement in the form of a protocol is to be ratified in the future.

[29] See Art. 24(1) TEU.

[30] 'Opt-outs' in the area of freedom, security and justice – which were introduced by the Maastricht and Amsterdam Treaties for the UK, Ireland and Denmark – have been maintained and extended to police and judicial cooperation in criminal matters.

[31] The revised Art. 48(6) TEU foresees a unanimous decision by the European Council and ratification by all member states according to their respective constitutional requirements, but no Convention and no Intergovernmental Conference.

Economic and Monetary Union, the area of freedom, security and justice, the environment, agriculture and competition. Other important changes could certainly be introduced *within* the Treaty framework, e.g. through an increasing use of enhanced cooperation, inter-institutional agreements among the EU institutions, political decisions or changes to the internal rules of procedure that apply to the institutions. Further developments could also come from agreements outside the EU Treaties that may subsequently be 'imported' at a later stage. In addition, the impact of actual institutional practices and the interpretation of the Treaty provisions by the European Court of Justice should not be underestimated.

3.   The EU institutions and the political system

The EU has the following institutions:[32]

- the European Parliament

- the European Council

- the Council of Ministers

- the European Commission

- the Court of Justice of the European Union

- the European Central Bank, and

- the Court of Auditors.

The three main institutions of the EU – referred to as the 'institutional triangle' – have traditionally been the European Commission (representing the Union's interests), the Council of Ministers (representing the different member states) and the European Parliament (representing EU citizens).[33]

---

[32] See also Art. 13 TEU.

[33] For more details on all EU institutions and their functioning, see E. Bomberg, J. Peterson and A. Stubb, *The European Union: How Does it Work?*, Oxford: Oxford University Press, 2008; see also D. Dinan, *Ever Closer Union: An Introduction to European Integration*, 4th edition, London: Palgrave Macmillan, 2010; and N. Nugent, *The Government and Politics of the European Union*, 7th edition, London: Palgrave Macmillan, 2010.

With the Treaty of Lisbon the European Council (consisting of the heads of state and government of the member states together with its permanent President and the President of the European Commission) has also been granted institutional status. As such it has its own rules of procedure and a (small) budget line.

While the European Court of Justice and the European Court of Auditors already had the status of EU institutions, the European Central Bank is newly featured on the list, but it retains its own legal personality and independence vis-à-vis the other institutions and member states.

3.1   The European Council

The European Council[34] is the institution through which the heads of state and government plus its permanent President and the European Commission President meet at least four times a year (the European summits). In contrast to the Council of Ministers, strictly speaking the European Council has no legislative powers, as its main task is to provide political guidance from the highest political level.[35] Rather than a legislator, the European Council's function is that of a political instigator. As such it is meant to provide the Union with the necessary impetus for its development and to define the general political guidelines of the EU. Political issues of a long-term perspective – such as the multi-annual budget or enlargement – are usually decided at the European Council level. In practice, it also acts as a political mediator among the configurations of the Council of Ministers, particularly when issues of a cross-sectoral or horizontal character are decided or as a decision-making body of last resort, in cases where the Council of Ministers fails to agree.

With the Treaty of Lisbon the European Council has not only received the status of an institution, but also a permanent President,

---

[34] The Council of Ministers and the European Council are not to be confused with the Council of Europe, which is a completely different international organisation that is not part of the EU's institutional framework (see appendix 1).

[35] See Art. 15(1) TEU: "The European Council shall provide the Union with the necessary impetus for its development and shall define the general political directions and priorities thereof."

elected for a term of two and a half years (renewable once). The Treaty of Lisbon has thus ended the six-monthly rotation of a head of state or government at the helm of the European Council and replaced it with a position that performs this function on a 'full-time' basis. The position is currently held by former Belgian Prime Minister Herman Van Rompuy. Since he has no staff of his own except his cabinet and spokespersons, the President relies on the Council Secretariat, under the authority of its Secretary-General, to assist him in carrying out his duties. The President chairs European summits and has to facilitate consensus within the European Council. He must ensure the preparation and continuity of the work of the European Council in cooperation with the European Commission President and he represents the EU externally at the level of heads of state and government for matters covered by the CFSP, although "without prejudice to the powers of the High Representative".[36] In view of the rather soft Treaty provisions, it is clear that the actual influence of this position derives from its agenda-setting power and the political skills of the person in office.

3.2 The Council of Ministers

In the Council of Ministers, national representatives meet in ten different configurations, depending on the policy issue, e.g. environmental ministers for environmental legislation, economic ministers for the internal market, and agricultural ministers for the common agricultural policy.[37] All the Council formations are presided by the member state holding the six-month rotating presidency, with the exception of the Foreign Affairs Council, which has been presided over by the High Representative since the Treaty of Lisbon entered into force (Box 1).[38]

---

[36] See Art. 15(6) TEU.

[37] For an overview, see "Council configurations", on the website of the Council of the European Union (http://www.consilium.europa.eu/showPage.asp?id=427&lang=en&mode=g).

[38] When trade issues are discussed, the Foreign Affairs Council continues to be presided by the rotating presidency.

Box 1. A new EU foreign policy chief supported by a new foreign service

The Treaty of Lisbon has merged the two positions of High Representative for Foreign Affairs and Security Policy on the one hand and Vice President of the European Commission in charge of the external relations portfolio on the other. The first appointee for this new 'double-hatted' position is Baroness Catherine Ashton (since 1 December 2009). The High Representative is appointed by the European Council, acting by a qualified majority and with the agreement of the President of the European Commission, while the Vice President is appointed as a member of the College of Commissioners, which includes a hearing before the European Parliament.

The position of Vice President of the European Commission entails the responsibilities incumbent on the European Commission in external relations and for coordinating other aspects of the Union's external action to ensure consistency.

The position of High Representative comes with the responsibility for conducting the CFSP, chairing the Foreign Affairs Council, submitting the necessary proposals and receiving executive mandates from the Council. The same applies to the common security and defence policy.

The High Representative represents the Union on matters relating to the CFSP, in conjunction with the President of the European Council (with the latter doing so at the level of heads of state and government). One can thus normally expect the High Representative to represent the EU on matters dealt with by foreign ministers. When for instance the US President and Secretary of State visit the EU, it can be expected that the US President would be welcomed by the Presidents of the European Commission and the European Council. The US Secretary of State would be welcomed by the High Representative. Before the entry into force of the Lisbon Treaty, the EU was represented at the highest level by the President of the European Commission as well as the president/prime minister of the member state holding the rotating presidency of the Council. At the level of foreign ministers the EU was represented by the foreign minister of the member state holding the rotating EU presidency.

Box 1. cont'd

The external representation of the Union on issues other than CFSP has not fundamentally changed: concerning EU policies the European Commission normally represents the EU (i.e. the President at the level of heads of state and government and the relevant Commissioner at the ministerial level). For those aspects of external policy that remain a national competence but which are touched by international negotiations involving the EU as a whole (and which do not belong to the CFSP), there is no general agreement on who should represent the EU externally. In those situations the representation is decided on case-by-case basis and usually involves a joint representation of stakeholders (the Commission and Member states, potentially the High Representative) under leadership of either the European Commission, the rotating presidency of the Council, the High Representative. In some specific situations, however, other forms of representation can be envisaged.

In fulfilling the mandate, the High Representative is to be assisted by the European External Action Service (EEAS), comprising officials from the European Commission and the General Secretariat of the Council as well as the diplomatic services of the member states. The organisation and functioning of this service have been established by the Council, acting on a proposal from the High Representative, after consulting Parliament and obtaining the consent of the European Commission (Art. 27(3) TEU). The Council adopted a decision on 26 July 2010 after difficult negotiations involving the High Representative, the Council, the European Commission and the European Parliament (so-called 'quadrilogues'). To become operational, the EEAS has also required changes to the financial and the staff regulations, as well as an amended budget. The EEAS was officially launched on 1 December 2010, a year after the entry into force of the Treaty of Lisbon.

The Council of Ministers remains the primary law-making body of the EU, although the number of areas where it has to share this competence with the European Parliament (in the framework of the ordinary legislative procedure, formerly referred to as 'co-decision') has grown continually with each treaty reform. The Treaty of Lisbon has given the legislative competences of the European Parliament another boost by increasing the share of legislation adopted by the ordinary legislative procedure from an estimated 80% under the Treaty of Nice to about 95% under the Treaty of Lisbon. As noted earlier, the entire domain of CFSP remains excluded, however.

One of the Council configurations is the General Affairs Council (GAC). It is composed of the 27 foreign ministers or state secretaries for EU affairs of the member states and meets at least monthly. As the name suggests, it deals with general and horizontal matters of the EU. As such it discusses EU institutional issues, enlargement and the multi-annual budget. Another important Council configuration is the Economic and Financial Affairs Council (Ecofin), where for instance the EU's annual budget is discussed.[39] Altogether there are nearly 100 meetings of all the Council configurations per year.

Unlike the European Council, the Council of Ministers continues to be chaired by a presidency that rotates among member states on a six-monthly basis. The only exception is the Foreign Affairs Council and its preparatory bodies, which are chaired by the High Representative for the CFSP or her staff. A strengthening of the rotating system has been envisaged through 'team presidencies', according to which three subsequent presidencies work closely together in their programming to ensure consistency in the Council's work.

The member state holding the rotating presidency has two nationals at the negotiation table: one to chair the meeting and represent the Council and one to defend the national interest of the member state. Generally, the presidency avoids pushing its national objectives and rather attempts to achieve a consensus among all countries. As its term is short, the presidency often relies heavily on the Council Secretariat in Brussels. The Council Secretariat briefs the presidency, helps to prepare the agendas and reports on progress. The Council Secretariat is managed by the Secretary-General. With the Treaty of Lisbon, most of its foreign policy tasks have been transferred from Directorate E –

---

[39] When the Ecofin Council examines dossiers related to the euro and EMU, the representatives of the member states whose currency is not the euro do not take part in the vote of the Council. Ecofin meetings are preceded by those of the 'Eurogroup', which is composed of the ministers from member states whose currency is the euro and which deals with issues relating to EMU. The Eurogroup is an informal body that is not a configuration of the Council.

External and Political-Military Affairs of the General Secretariat to the European External Action Service.

Meetings of the Council of Ministers are supported by a wealth of preparatory bodies that together function as a filter. At a first stage, national civil servants and diplomats meet to deal with mostly technical and uncontroversial issues. They meet within the senior committees and working parties, of which around 160 have been established with the aim of reaching agreement on as many aspects as possible.[40] Important senior committees include the Political and Security Committee (PSC), the Standing Committee on Internal Security (COSI) introduced by the Treaty of Lisbon to promote and strengthen cooperation on internal security within the EU, the Trade Policy Committee[41] and the Special Committee on Agriculture. Among the working parties, the Environment Working Party stands out, as it meets about three days a week and deals with a large number of environmental files. With the exception of CFSP issues, chaired mostly by staff of the High Representative, almost all meetings in the Council are chaired by the rotating presidency (Table 4) and take place according to a fixed seating order (Figure 3).

Only those aspects that cannot be agreed among member state experts (so-called 'B items') are then referred to the next level: COREPER, the Committee of Permanent Representatives to the EU, which actually consists of two separate committees. COREPER II is composed of the permanent representatives of the EU member states,

---

[40] See L. Van Schaik et al., *Policy Coherence for Development in the Council: Strategies for the way forward*, Centre for European Policy Studies, Brussels, 2006; see also S. Hagemann and J. De Clerck-Sachsse, *Old Rules, New Game: Decision-making in the Council of Ministers after the 2004 Enlargement*, CEPS Special Report, Centre for European Policy Studies, Brussels, March 2007.

[41] Before the Treaty of Lisbon this committee was known as the 'Article 133 Committee', named after the treaty article by which it was created (this article has since become Art. 207, but the committee is no longer named after the article).

normally ambassadors who head the permanent representations[42] of the member state to the EU and deal with external policies, negotiations on the EU budget and other sensitive issues. It is a close-knit group that meets once a week officially and even more frequently informally to discuss, for instance, foreign policy issues. COREPER I brings together the deputy permanent representatives and deals mostly with what was previously called first pillar policies, e.g. the single market and all its technical and regulatory aspects.

Table 4. Council presidency – Order of rotation

Year	Period	Country	Year	Period	Member state
2010	July-Dec	Belgium	2015	July-Dec	Luxembourg
2011	Jan-June	Hungary	2016	Jan-June	Netherlands
2011	July-Dec	Poland	2016	July-Dec	Slovakia
2012	Jan-June	Denmark	2017	Jan-June	Malta
2012	July-Dec	Cyprus	2017	July-Dec	UK
2013	Jan-June	Ireland	2018	Jan-June	Estonia
2013	July-Dec	Lithuania	2018	July-Dec	Bulgaria
2014	Jan-June	Greece	2019	Jan-June	Austria
2014	July-Dec	Italy	2019	July-Dec	Romania
2015	Jan-June	Latvia	2020	Jan-June	Finland

Source: Council Decision of 1 January 2007 determining the order in which the office of President of the Council shall be held, published in the *Official Journal* on 4.1.2007.

---

[42] Permanent representations are similar to embassies, but they are diplomatic entities in relation to the EU as a whole and not to any specific country. In addition, non-EU member states usually have specific diplomats working on EU issues in 'missions' (e.g. the US mission to the EU).

Figure 3. The seating order in the Council (except for the Foreign Affairs Council)

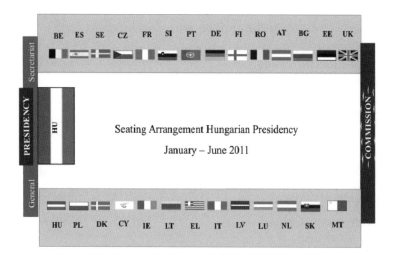

Source: Netherlands Institute of International Relations Clingendael.

In areas where unanimity is required (e.g. taxation), decisions tend to be based on the lowest common denominator. In cases where qualified majority voting applies, however, national governments are forced to make real compromises. Traditionally preference is always given to a consensus acceptable to every country, not least because legislative measures have to be implemented and enforced by all member states. Actual voting has continued to be the exception, but the mere *possibility* of proceeding to a vote (known as the 'shadow of the vote') has often been sufficient to make member states seek compromise. Yet how the consensus mode of the Council of Ministers can or will be preserved in an enlarged Union is an issue of debate.

The Treaty of Lisbon has made significant changes to the system for calculating the *qualified majority* within the Council and the areas to which it applies. According to this 'double majority' system, a majority will be obtained if at least 55% of member states that represent at least 65% of the EU's population are in favour of a proposal. Still, the new voting system will replace the current rules only from 2014 onwards. Moreover, there will be a period until 2017 when each member state can demand that the current rules be applied instead of the double-majority system. The voting system was one of the most contested elements in the negotiations on the Treaty of Lisbon, as certain countries (e.g. Germany) are set to gain voting power under the new system, while others (e.g. Poland and Spain) are set to lose. The Polish government in particular was opposed to the new system until additional clauses were agreed that would guarantee further negotiations if a certain number of countries – even if not constituting a blocking minority – are against a proposal (inspired by the 'Ioannina compromise').[43]

The change to a new voting system is seen as especially important as the Treaty of Lisbon has increased the number of cases where national vetoes have been abolished. Qualified majority voting has been introduced to 44 new cases:

- 24 cases relate to issues formerly requiring unanimity, notably concerning implementation of provisions on the area of freedom, security and justice (border controls, asylum, immigration, Eurojust and Europol);[44] proposals under the CFSP made by the High Representative for Foreign Affairs and Security Policy at the request of the European Council; the arrangements for monitoring the exercise of the European Commission's executive powers (also

---

[43] The Ioannina compromise refers to a decision taken at an informal meeting of foreign ministers in the Greek city of Ioannina on 29 March 1994, laying down that if members of the Council representing between 23 votes (the old blocking minority threshold) and 26 votes (the new threshold) express their intention to oppose the taking of a decision by the Council by qualified majority, the Council will do all within its power, within a reasonable space of time, to reach a satisfactory solution that can be adopted by at least 68 votes out of 87 (*source:* "Europa Glossary").

[44] Eurojust is a judicial cooperation body. Europol is a European law enforcement agency for improving cooperation of the EU law enforcement authorities.

known as 'comitology');[45] and establishing special tribunals and amending parts of the statutes of the Court of Justice and of the European System of Central Banks; and

- 20 cases concern new legal bases, for example on the principles and conditions for operating services of general economic interest,[46] and the arrangements for protecting intellectual property, energy, humanitarian aid and civil protection.

3.3   The European Commission

3.3.1 Composition

The European Commission that took office in February 2010 consists of one Commissioner per member state and has 27 members, including those from Romania and Bulgaria, which joined the EU in January 2007. The European Commission's President José Manuel Barroso was appointed by the European Council and confirmed by the European Parliament for a second term. The rules for the appointment under the Treaty of Lisbon make a link between the (party-) political background of the person, who the European Council proposes on the basis of qualified majority and in view of the outcome of the European parliamentary elections. The presidential nominee must then be elected by the European Parliament. The position of the European Commission President has been further strengthened, giving him more powers over his colleagues than in the past.[47]

---

[45] Comitology describes the EU system of delegating detailed implementing measures to the executive through committees that consist of member states and are chaired by the European Commission.

[46] In Eurojargon, services of general economic interest refer to those that are to be provided even where the market is not sufficiently profitable for the supply of such services.

[47] For example, the European Commission President can request a member of the European Commission to resign, even without the approval of the other Commissioners (Art. 17(6), second subparagraph TEU).

Commissioners are appointed by prime ministers in agreement with the designated Commission President, but need to be confirmed as a team (the 'College') by a vote of consent from the European Parliament. Commissioners are appointed for a term of five years, in line with the Parliament's tenure. Each Commissioner, including the President, has one vote when the European Commission votes. The voting rule applied on such occasions is a simple majority (>50%) and the vote of the European Commission President decides if there is a tie. In reality, however, the College reportedly has not proceeded to a vote since 2004.

The European Commission is collectively responsible for its decisions and Commissioners are pledged to serve the EU interest. They are not supposed to take any instructions from a national government or other external actor. Commissioners nonetheless have an important role in keeping the link between the European Commission and their national publics, and therefore provide a crucial clearing-house for differences between the respective member states and the Commission.

Concerning the size of the College, the Treaty of Lisbon actually foresaw reducing the number of Commissioners to two-thirds of the number of member states from 2014 onwards (based on a system of equal rotation among all nationalities). But the measure to reduce the College was dropped, in accordance with the conditions set by the Irish government in order for the latter to organise a new referendum on the Lisbon Treaty. The new Treaty contains a provision according to which the European Council can decide unanimously to keep the rule of one Commissioner per member state.

The cabinets of Commissioners play an important role within the European Commission. Each cabinet has about eight members who keep the Commissioner updated on specific issues and brief the Commissioner when a discussion is scheduled for a particular European Commission meeting. Separately and before the Commissioners meet, the *chefs de cabinet* (comparable with heads of private offices) meet under the chairmanship of the Secretary-General of the European Commission to prepare the regular Commission meetings, which generally take place on Wednesdays.[48] Each Commissioner selects his or her own cabinet. In the past, cabinets were dominated by members with the same nationality as the Commissioner, which gave rise to complaints about the influence of national interests in the European Commission. As a consequence, during the Prodi Commission (1999–2004) the practice of selecting half of the cabinet staff from nationalities other than the Commissioner's was encouraged. This practice has been further extended, under both the Barroso I (2004–10) and Barroso II Commissions (2010– to the present).

The services of the European Commission are divided into Directorates-General (DGs), which are subdivided into Policy, External Relations, General Services and Internal Services DGs (see Box 2). With the establishment of the European External Action Service, however, almost the entire DG RELEX (External Relations) and parts of DG DEV (Development) have been transferred to this new service. The Legal Service deserves particular mention; it gives its legal opinion on planned decisions and legislative initiatives. It is rare that the opinion of the Legal Service is disregarded. Another important service is that of the European Commission's Secretariat-General, which is responsible for horizontal coordination and communication within the Commission. The Secretary-General is one of the most senior officials of the European Commission and chairs key committee meetings.

The number of DGs and Commissioners is not the same, as several DGs work for more than one Commissioner. In some cases one Commissioner is responsible for more than one DG, while in others there are several Commissioners working with one DG.

Before proposals go to the cabinets and Commissioners for approval they undergo an 'inter-service' consultation, in which all related DGs are consulted on draft versions of legislative proposals. At the same time, an integrated impact assessment process is conducted, which includes a cost-benefit analysis and a justification for the choice of policy instrument in comparison with alternative policy options.

---

[48] During plenary sessions of the European Parliament in Strasbourg, these take place on Tuesdays.

Box 2. Directorates-General of the European Commission

Policy DGs

Agriculture and Rural Development (AGRI)

Climate Action (CLIMA)

Competition (COMP)

Economic and Financial Affairs (ECFIN)

Education and Culture (EAC)

Employment, Social Affairs and Equal Opportunities (EMPL)

Energy (ENER)

Enterprise and Industry (ENTR)

Environment (ENV)

Maritime Affairs and Fisheries (MARE)

Health and Consumers (SANCO)

Home Affairs (HOME)

Information Society and Media (INFSO)

Internal Market and Services (MARKT)

Joint Research Centre (JRC)

Justice (JUST)

Regional Policy (REGIO)

Research (RTD)

Taxation and Customs Union (TAXUD)

Mobility and Transport (MOVE)

External relations DGs

Enlargement (ELARG)

EuropeAid Development and Cooperation (DEVCO)

Humanitarian Aid and Civil Protection (ECHO)

Trade (TRADE)

DG RELEX (External Relations) ceased to exist, with most of its staff having been transferred to the European External Action Service (EEAS) on 1 January 2011.

The Foreign Policy Instruments Service (FPIS) manages EU external cooperation programmes for which the European Commission continues to be responsible; the staff are co-located with the EEAS and report to the High Representative in her capacity as a Vice President of the European Commission.

General services DGs

Communication (COMM)

European Anti-Fraud Office (OLAF)

Eurostat

Publications Office (OP)

Secretariat-General (SG)

Internal services

Budget (BUDG)

Bureau of European Policy Advisers (BEPA)

Informatics (DIGIT)

Infrastructure and Logistics (OIB/OIL)

Internal Audit Service (IAS)

Interpretation (SCIC)

Legal Service (SJ)

Human Resources and Security (HR)

Translation (DGT)

Source: European Commission, "Departments (Directorate-Generals) and services", 7 December 2010 (http://ec.europa.eu/dgs_en.htm).

In the past, appointments of European Commission staff followed a rough quota system with nationality being an important aspect. Entering the European Commission and other institutions typically required passing the 'concours' or competition, which essentially tested knowledge. Recruitment has since been bundled into the European Personnel Selection Office (EPSO), a kind of assessment centre with a stronger focus on competence and skills to ensure that applicants better match the job requirements. The process remains highly competitive and can easily take more than a year. The European Commission employs around 20,000 officials directly, not including translators. Besides permanent staff, it also employs temporary and contract agents for much of its work.

3.3.2 Functions

The European Commission has five basic functions:

- the right and duty of initiating Union action and legislation;
- the role of guardian of the Treaties;
- responsibility for the implementation of Union decisions;
- decision-making authority in the field of competition policy; and
- external representation of the EU, with the exception of the CFSP and other cases explicitly provided for in the Treaties.[49]

i) The right of initiative

With few exceptions, the European Commission has a monopoly – at least in the strict legal sense – on initiating legislation (i.e. the right of initiative), although it often takes action after it has been asked to do so by the European Council. The Treaty also gives the Council and the European Parliament the possibility to request the European Commission to take action. Furthermore, with the new instrument of the European Citizens' Initiative, a million EU citizens can 'invite' the European Commission to make a legislative proposal. Yet in all cases

---

[49] See S. Kurpas, C. Grøn and P.M. Kaczyński, *The European Commission after enlargement: Does more add up to less?*, CEPS Special Report, Centre for European Policy Studies, Brussels, February 2008.

the ultimate decision (and responsibility) on whether to take action remains with the European Commission. Not least the smaller member states feel that this exclusive right of initiative safeguards their interests best, as the European Commission is meant to be the advocate of the 'common EU interest'.

The right of initiative makes the European Commission the engine for integration and provides the main source of its power. With very few exceptions the Council and the European Parliament can only decide on the basis of a European Commission proposal.[50] This gives the European Commission a key role in the identification of common interests and makes it an important interlocutor for stakeholders and interest groups (see chapter 10). To plan its initiatives the European Commission used to develop a strategic programme for the year ahead, the Annual Policy Strategy (APS), which it presented in February of the preceding year and which translated into the operational work programme of the European Commission. In 2010 the European Commission ceased presenting an APS, and instead the Commission President gave a state of the union speech before the European Parliament. The occasion coincided with a letter he had sent to MEPs in which he outlined the European Commission's main policy initiatives to be taken up in the Commission's work programme for 2011. This innovation has taken place against the background of the changes introduced by the Treaty of Lisbon and the new framework agreement between the European Commission and the European Parliament.[51]

---

[50] In the area of the former third pillar (i.e. police and judicial cooperation on criminal matters) an initiative can also be put forward by a quarter of the member states (Art. 76 TFEU). In the area of CFSP the adoption of legislative acts is excluded (Art. 24(1) TEU), but non-legislative initiatives or proposals can be submitted to the Council by any member state, by the High Representative or by the High Representative with the European Commission's support (Art. 30(1) TEU).

[51] With the revisions made by the Treaty of Lisbon, the EU Treaty now explicitly mentions that the European Commission shall initiate the Union's annual and multi-annual programmes with a view to achieving inter-institutional agreements (Art. 17(1) TEU).

Another novelty is the political guidelines that Commission President Barroso presented in September 2009 in the context of obtaining the European Parliament's approval for a second term in office. In this document Barroso outlined his policy priorities in order to find the necessary support in the Parliament.[52]

In its role as the engine for integration, the European Commission consults extensively with member states (in particular with the presidency of the Council of Ministers, which decides upon its agenda), the European Parliament and stakeholders. In addition, the European Commission is responsible for the budget and its execution. In that sense the European Commission is a political manager with a unique European outlook that balances the different national and political interests coming from the other institutions, member states and interest groups.

ii) The guardian of the Treaties

As guardian of the Treaties, the European Commission is responsible for the proper implementation and the enforcement of Union law. It polices the administration of EU law and assigns judgements against governments (including fines) or individuals who violate the Treaties. As a last resort, it can take offenders to the European Court of Justice (see Box 3). In the past this has been mainly the case for violations of legislation related to the internal market. The European Commission takes a tough stance if member states fail to transpose, implement or enforce Union legislation. Enforcement follows a standardised procedure.

---

[52] See J.M. Barroso, *Political Guidelines for the Next Commission*, European Commission, Brussels, 2009 (http://ec.europa.eu/commission_2010-2014/president/pdf/press_20090903_en.pdf).

Box 3. Infringement procedure

The infringement procedure is regulated by Art. 258 of the Treaty on the Functioning of the European Union (TFEU):

> If the Commission considers that a Member State has failed to fulfil an obligation under the Treaties, it shall deliver a reasoned opinion on the matter after giving the State concerned the opportunity to submit its observations. If the State concerned does not comply with the opinion within the period laid down by the Commission, the latter may bring the matter before the Court of Justice of the European Union.

Detailed rules of procedure have been drawn up as the European Commission's internal rules have been established by legal practice or case law. Important features are the opening of the procedure by a letter of formal notice, and the possibility for the concerned member state to submit its observations on the identified problem within a given time limit. The purpose of this 'pre-litigation phase' is also to enable the respective member state to conform voluntarily to the requirements of Union law. The European Commission will then issue a reasoned opinion. It is based on the letter of formal notice and gives a detailed statement of the reasons that have led the European Commission to assume that the member state concerned has not fulfilled its obligations under the Treaties or secondary EU legislation. Referral by the European Commission to the European Court of Justice (ECJ) opens the actual litigation procedure. The ECJ will decide whether there has been an infringement and what penalty may apply.*

With the Treaty of Lisbon, the infringement procedure has been reinforced by introducing two new features:

- For infringement proceedings based on the failure of a member state to notify the national transposition measure of a directive, the European Commission has been given the possibility to propose penalty payments or a lump sum already at the stage of the first referral to the Court (Art. 260(3) TFEU).

- A reasoned opinion from the European Commission for cases of non-compliance with ECJ judgments is no longer necessary before the Commission can take the member state again to the Court (Art. 260(2) TFEU).

Box 3. cont'd

Of the 143 ECJ judgments in 2009 concerning the failure of a member state to fulfil its obligations, the Court declared infringements in 134 cases, with the action being dismissed in only 9 cases. The average length of an infringement procedure closed in 2009 by the ECJ was 17.1 months.**

Penalties are calculated as daily fines based on a complex formula, including the seriousness and length of the breach and the ability to pay, expressed as per capita income.

* See the European Commission's website, "Application of EU law", "Infringements of EU Law", 1 March 2011 (http://ec.europa.eu/community_law/infringements/infringements_en.htm).

** See the website of the Court of Justice of the European Union, *Annual Report 2009*(http://curia.europa.eu/jcms/upload/docs/application/pdf/2010-05/ra09_stat_cour_final_en.pdf).

---

iii)   Implementation of Union policy

In this area of the European Commission's executive powers – traditionally referred to as comitology – the Treaty of Lisbon has brought important innovations. It has introduced a distinction between delegated acts on the one hand ("non-legislative acts of general application to supplement or amend certain non-essential elements of the legislative act", Art. 290 TFEU) and mere implementing acts on the other (Art. 291 TFEU). A typical delegated act would be amending an annex listing the items (e.g. goods or species) to which the respective legislative act applies, while a typical implementing act would deal with the purely technical aspects of implementing the legislative act. In the past, the division between acts falling under the different comitology procedures has occasionally been somewhat blurred and the new system holds potential for greater clarity.

- **Delegated acts** are subject to the *ex-post* control of both branches of the legislator, i.e. the European Parliament and the Council of Ministers, on an equal footing. Delegated acts prepared and adopted by the European Commission can only enter into force if no objection has been expressed by either the European Parliament or the Council. The legislator also has the right to revoke the European Commission's delegated powers at a later stage.[53]

- On **implementing Acts**, Art. 291 TFEU stipulates that where uniform conditions for the implementation of legally binding acts are needed, implementation can be undertaken by the European Commission or exceptionally by the Council (see Figure 4). Art. 291 TFEU – unlike Art. 290 TFEU on delegated acts – is not a self-executing provision. The regulation on the implementing acts sets out rules and general principles concerning the mechanisms for control by member states of the European Commission's exercise of implementing powers.[54]

---

[53] On 9 December 2009 the European Commission adopted a Communication concerning delegated acts (Implementation of Article 290 of the Treaty on the Functioning of the European Union, COM(2009) 673, Brussels, 9 December 2009) to ensure a clear understanding with the European Parliament and Council on how to use delegated acts. Agreement on a "Common Understanding" among the three institutions was reached at the end of 2010.

[54] To this end, on 16 February 2011 the European Parliament and the Council adopted Regulation (EU) No. 182/2011 laying down the rules and general principles concerning mechanisms for control by Member States of the Commission's exercise of implementing powers (2010/0051/COD). The new regulation replaced the 'Comitology Decision' adopted by the Council in 1999 and amended in 2006. Yet beyond their initial role in adopting the regulation, Art. 291 TFEU does not foresee the institutional involvement of either the Parliament or the Council in the preparation or adoption of implementing acts, as the provision explicitly refers to the "member states" in this regard. The new regulation foresees only two procedures ("advisory" and "examination") and an automatic alignment of existing comitology procedures (advisory, management and regulatory) with the new regulation: all existing advisory procedures are to remain advisory, while all the management and regulatory procedures are to become "examination" procedures. Concerning delegated acts, such an automatism does not exist, but the European Commission has committed to aligning old acts now falling under the provisions for delegated acts (i.e. most comitology acts adopted by the regulatory procedure with scrutiny) until the end of 2014.

Figure 4.New comitology rules (Art. 191 TFEU)

Commission proposes a draft implementing act	

if the draft act is of general scope, or is specific and relates to
- programmes with substantial implications
- agriculture and fisheries
- environment, protection of the health of humans, animals and plants
- trade
- taxation

as a general rule, for all other draft acts

Advisory procedure committee, composed of member states' representatives and chaired by the Commission, **delivers its opinion by simple majority**

Examination procedure committee, composed of member states' representatives and chaired by the Commission, **delivers its opinion by qualified majority**

Commission adopts the act, taking the utmost account of the committee's opinion

positive opinion:

Commission adopts draft act

no opinion:

Commission may adopt draft act unless

- it concerns taxation, financial services, the protection of humans, animals or plants health, or definitive multilateral safeguard measures
- the basic act so provides
- a simple majority of the committee opposes it.

In these three cases the Commission may either submit the draft act within 1 month to the *appeal committee* or submit to the committee within 2 months an amended text.[1]

If the draft act concerns the adoption of definitive antidumping or countervailing measures and a simple majority opposes it the Commission must consult the member states and submit the draft act to the *appeal committee*.

negative opinion:

- Commission submits draft act within 1 month to the *appeal committee* or
- submits within 2 months an amended draft act.[1]

Appeal committee, composed of representatives of the member states at appropriate level and chaired by the Commission, **delivers its opinion by qualified majority**[2]

positive opinion:

Commission adopts draft act

no opinion:

Commission may adopt draft act, unless it concerns definitive multilateral safeguard measures where in the absence of a positive opinion voted by qualified majority the Commission must not adopt the draft act

negative opinion:

Commission must not adopt draft act

Source: "Council adopts new 'comitology' rules", Council of the European Union, 6378/11 Presse 23, Brussels, 14 February 2011.

Comitology committees are relatively similar to Council working groups as they are composed of EU member state representatives and can sometimes resort to voting to take decisions. Yet unlike Council working groups, they are not chaired by representatives of the Council presidency, but by the European Commission.[55] Comitology has at times been viewed as going beyond decision-making on 'implementation details', posing questions about the legitimacy and transparency of decision-making in the European Union. The new regime as outlined above can be understood as a reaction to this criticism, as those acts that go beyond mere implementation (i.e. delegated acts) are now subject to a veto of both the Council and the European Parliament and both institutions can also revoke the delegation to the European Commission.

iv) Own decision-making authority in the field of competition policy

In most policy areas, the European Commission only performs a supervisory role to check whether member states implement and enforce policies properly. With regard to competition policy, the European Commission is nonetheless directly and immediately responsible for taking decisions on the activities of companies active in more than one EU member state. For instance, it can prohibit or alter mergers of large multinationals[56] or impose very significant fines for violating EU competition rules (e.g. collusion or the abuse of a dominant position) by companies operating in the EU, irrespective of whether of EU or foreign origin. The European Commission can also block member states from handing out illegal subsidies to companies, or in cases where subsidies have already been paid, force the repayment (Box 4).

---

[55] A list of comitology committees can be found on the European Commission's "Comitology Register" (http://ec.europa.eu/transparency/regcomitology/index.cfm).

[56] In reality and according to procedural rules, the European Commission consults extensively with member states before taking a decision.

Box 4. An evolving EU competition policy

Over the years, the EU's competition authorities have gradually increased their influence. There have been a number of high-profile cases where the European Commission has blocked mergers (including of firms headquartered outside the EU), fined companies for violation of competition rules or forced member states to repay illegal state aid, i.e. subsidies to companies. Controversial cases or setbacks in the courts have triggered reform and improved international cooperation.

Typically, the EU fights restrictive practices and cartels, and it hands down significant fines, often in the hundreds of millions, to companies in various sectors. The record fine to date has amounted to over €1 billion. In the field of competition policy, the EU has special investigative rights to undertake raids in conjunction with member states' authorities.

Other high-profile cases involve mergers. For example, the European Commission has blocked the mergers of companies headquartered in the US (i.e. the proposed GE–Honeywell merger in early 2000) or forced significant concessions (i.e. the Boeing–McDonnell Douglas merger) after the US competition authorities had already cleared the cases.

Box 4 cont'd

The negative verdicts by the European Court (of First Instance) – under the Treaty of Lisbon now called the 'General Court' – on three Commission decisions blocking mergers (i.e. the respective mergers of Airtours–First Choice, Tetra Laval–Sidel and Schneider–Legrand) triggered an in-depth procedural revamp of how mergers are examined.

Another controversial area is control of state aid by member states, which potentially distorts competition in the EU internal market. In principle, all state aid – i.e. government subsidies over a certain threshold – need to be notified to the European Commission, which decides whether the subsidies are lawful or not. This regularly leads to high-profile cases between the European Commission's competition authorities and the member states.

---

v)   External representation of the European Union

The European Commission represents the EU externally on all matters of EU competence other than in the area of CFSP or other fields explicitly provided for in the Treaties. Where Union competence is exclusive, as in the area of trade, it is the lead negotiator of the EU. At the time of writing, the European Commission was in disagreement with the Council over the interpretation of the Treaty of Lisbon concerning external representation in international negotiations on matters falling under 'shared competence' (i.e. issues where both EU and national policies co-exist).[57] Both the European Commission President and the President of the European Council take part in the meetings of the G-8, the gatherings of leaders of the 7 richest countries and Russia, and the G-20. With the Treaty of Lisbon the delegations of the European Commission that exist all over the world have become EU delegations. Administratively they are to become part of the European External Action Service, while staff dealing with issues falling within the European Commission's competence (e.g. trade) continue to report to the Commission. (External representation is dealt with in greater detail in chapter 11.)

3.4 The European Parliament

The European Parliament's influence on legislation has grown steadily during the various treaty revisions, from the Single European Act to the Maastricht, Amsterdam, Nice and now the Lisbon Treaty. The European Parliament has taken on the role of co-legislator on an equal footing with the Council of Ministers in most policy areas. It also plays a significant role in the budget negotiations and has a veto right for most international agreements, including enlargement, through the consent procedure (i.e. the European Parliament cannot formally suggest any amendments, but it can approve or disapprove the text as a whole). Notably all agreements that cover policy fields falling under the ordinary legislative procedure or the consent procedure (see chapter 4) always require the consent of the European Parliament. For other areas, such as the CFSP and a limited number of issues in the field of agriculture and fisheries,[58] the Parliament is only involved in a consultative way. The resolutions that it issues in these fields can easily be set aside by the Council.

---

[57] As a consequence, the European Commission withdrew the draft negotiation directives for an international agreement on mercury that it had proposed to the Council.

[58] On fixing prices, levies, aid, quantitative limitations and the fixing and allocation of fishing opportunities, see Art. 43(3) TFEU.

The Parliament currently consists of 736 deputies or MEPs (see Table 3 above), as the 2009 elections took place under the old rules of the Treaty of Nice. Under the Treaty of Lisbon 751 deputies are foreseen and the additional MEPs should take office once the necessary provisions are in place.[59] MEPs are chosen on the basis of national lists (e.g. a German citizen residing in Germany can only vote for candidates who are on the list for a German party, but they do not need to be of German nationality). After the elections the national political parties join forces in European political groups. The Parliament decides by a majority of its members,[60] but – like the other EU institutions – it is a consensus-driven body. Despite the presence of two large political groups, the centre-right European People's Party (Christian Democrats and Conservatives) and the centre-left Socialist and Democrats Party, neither is large enough to form a majority on its own (see Table 5). Hence, coalition building is a necessity to approve, reject or amend legislation.[61] Most of the legislation is discussed and shaped in

---

[59] As Germany is set to lose 3 MEPs under the Treaty of Lisbon compared with the Treaty of Nice (96 instead of 99), but all current MEPs have been elected under the Treaty of Nice for a full five-year term, the total number of MEPs will temporarily (i.e. for the rest of the 2009–14 parliamentary term) reach 754 when the additional 18 MEPs foreseen under the Treaty of Lisbon take office. As the Treaty only allows a maximum of 751, however, the Treaty must be changed in order to allow for the 18 MEPs to take office during the current parliamentary term. This Treaty change was agreed by all member states in July 2010, but at the time of writing the ratification process had not yet been concluded.

[60] In the framework of the ordinary legislative procedure, the European Parliament decides by a simple majority of all MEPs present at the plenary vote. Yet in the second reading, the European Parliament must decide by an absolute majority of its members. This creates an incentive to reach agreement during the first reading.

[61] Different winning coalitions are possible. According to "EU Vote Watch" (http://www.votewatch.eu) – a website monitoring the European Parliament – on economic issues the winning coalition consists of ALDE (liberal) and the EPP (centre-right), whereas on social issues and personal freedoms the EPP tends to give ground to the wider centre-left coalition of socialists/social democrats, liberals and greens. This would give the liberal group the role of 'kingmaker' in this European Parliament.

committees in which a restricted number of MEPs from different political parties and nationalities participate (Box 5). When the proposal from the committee is voted upon in the European Parliament's plenary session, most of the coalition building and horse-trading has already been done. Of particular importance therefore is the rapporteur, i.e. the MEP writing the report that contains amendments to the legislative proposal supported by a majority in his or her committee. This text is usually the basis for the vote in the plenary.

Table 5. Political groups in the European Parliament

Political group	Number of MEPs
Group of the European People's Party/Christian Democrats (EPP)	265
Group of the Progressive Alliance of Socialists and Democrats in the European Parliament (S&D)	186
Group of the Alliance of Liberals and Democrats for Europe (ALDE)	84
Group of the Greens/European Free Alliance (Greens/EFA)	55
European Conservatives and Reformists Group (ECR)	54
Confederal Group of the European United Left – Nordic Green Left (GEU/NGL)	35
Europe of Freedom and Democracy Group (EFD)	30
Non-attached members (NI)	27

Source: European Parliament (December 2009).

Box 5.The European Parliament: Committees and delegations

Foreign Affairs (AFET) with Human Rights (DROI) and Security and Defence (SEDE) Sub-committees

Development (DEVE)

International Trade (INTA)

Budget (BUDG)

Budgetary Control (CONT)

Economic and Monetary Affairs (ECON)

Employment and Social Affairs (EMPL)

Environment, Public Health and Food Safety (ENVI)

Industry, Research and Energy (ITRE)

Internal Market and Consumer Protection (IMCO)

Transport and Tourism (TRAN)

Regional Development (REGI)

Agriculture and Rural Development (AGRI)

Fisheries (PECH)

Culture and Education (CULT)

Legal Affairs (JURI)

Civil Liberties, Justice and Home Affairs (LIBE)

Constitutional Affairs (AFCO)

Women's Rights and Gender Equality (FEMM)

Petitions (PETI)

These can be complemented by special or temporary committees.

The committees are complemented with 35-40 joint parliamentary committees, cooperation committees or interparliamentary delegations with almost all major countries or regional blocs in Europe and beyond.

In addition, MEPS of different political groups create 'inter-groups' to advance specific issues.

In recent years, the European Parliament has acted with increasing self-confidence, for example on important files and issues like the chemicals directive REACH, the services directive, and the climate action and renewable energy package. The European Parliament has also been very self-confident about exercising the new powers it has obtained under the Treaty of Lisbon. Within a couple of weeks after the Treaty's entry into force Parliament threatened to veto a free trade agreement with South Korea and successfully demanded an additional safeguard regulation. It also rejected a first draft of the SWIFT agreement (concerning the access of US authorities to the banking data of EU citizens).

The hearings of Commissioners-designate have become another opportunity for the European Parliament to demonstrate its increased powers. As the European Parliament cannot send individual Commissioners home, it successfully threatened to veto the entire College of Commissioners in 2004, when a majority of socialists and liberals was not convinced by the hearing of the Commissioner-designate from Italy, Rocco Buttiglione. Similarly it threatened to reject the proposed College because of the Bulgarian candidate for Commissioner, Rumiana Jeleva, in 2009.

As an ultimate instrument vis-à-vis the European Commission, the European Parliament has a motion of censure for the Commission at its disposal. It has never actually censored a European Commission, but successfully threatened to do so in 1999, as a result of which the Santer Commission stepped down after allegations of fraud.

3.5   The Court of Justice of the European Union

The Court of Justice of the European Union – often referred to as the European Court of Justice (ECJ) – dates back to the ECSC Treaty of 1952 and it is located in Luxembourg. Its mission is to ensure the coherent interpretation and application of EU legislation across all member states. It is composed of one judge from each member state, but it usually sits as a Grand Chamber of thirteen judges or in chambers of five or three judges. The Court is assisted by eight advocates-general who present reasoned opinions on the cases brought before the Court. Judges and advocates-general are impartial and they are appointed by joint agreement among the member states for a term of six years (renewable).

In 1988 a Court of First Instance was created to help the ECJ cope with the large number of cases brought before it. With the Treaty of Lisbon it was renamed the General Court. It deals with cases brought by private individuals and companies as well as cases relating to competition law. The European Union Civil Service Tribunal (established in 2005) is responsible for disputes between the EU and its civil servants.

The following five kinds of cases are the most common:

- references for a preliminary ruling (Art. 267 TFEU),
- actions for failure to fulfil an obligation (Arts. 258 and 259 TFEU),
- actions for annulment (Art. 263 TFEU),
- actions for failure to act (Art. 265 TFEU), and
- actions for damages (Art. 268 TFEU).[62]

The Court has proved to be of crucial importance for the European integration process. In the past a series of Court rulings established the primacy of Union law over national law. This principle is implicit in the Treaties, but only the Court made it explicit.[63] The Court also established the direct applicability (or 'direct effect') of EU law.[64] As a consequence, Union law can directly impose obligations on individuals and likewise confer rights on them, which they can invoke before national courts and the ECJ. Hence, this 'direct effect' allows them to take advantage of Union provisions regardless of their transposition into national law. The common foreign and security policy remains largely excluded from the Court's jurisdiction. As regards the former third pillar (i.e. police and judicial cooperation on criminal matters) only very few limitations remain.[65]

---

[62] A more detailed explanation of all procedures can be found on the European Commission's website, "European institutions and bodies", "The Court of Justice" (http://europa.eu/institutions/inst/justice/index_en.htm).

[63] See Case 6/64, *Costa v. ENEL* [1964] ECR 585.

[64] See Case 26/62, *Van Gend & Loos v. Netherlands Inland Revenue Administration* [1963] ECR 1.

[65] The Court continues to have no jurisdiction on the validity and proportionality of police operations and measures taken by the member states

EU citizens and entities do not necessarily have to go to the Court in Luxembourg, as European law is safeguarded by national judges who look at earlier verdicts regarding possible violations of European law or put a prejudicial question to the European Court of Justice.

3.6 Other institutions and bodies

Other institutions and bodies include the following:

- The **Court of Auditors** in Luxembourg achieved the status of an institution with the Maastricht Treaty. It examines the accounts of the Union's revenue and expenditures and checks whether financial management is sound. It reports to the European Parliament.

- The **European Central Bank** (ECB) in Frankfurt gained institutional status with the Treaty of Lisbon, but it continues to retain its own legal personality and its independence vis-à-vis the other institutions and the member states. The ECB is in charge of the management of the EU's common currency.

- The **European Investment Bank** in Luxembourg provides low interest loans to poorer regions both within the Union and outside it (e.g. to developing countries from the African, Caribbean and Pacific region and the EU's candidate, associated and neighbourhood countries).

- The **European Economic and Social Committee** in Brussels has an advisory role and gives opinions on matters concerning the social partners (labour and employers organisations).

- The **Committee of the Regions** in Brussels is another EU advisory body that deals with issues of concern for the European regions. It was created by the Treaty of Maastricht.

---

to maintain law and order or to safeguard internal security. For acts adopted *prior* to the entry into force of the Lisbon Treaty (i.e. still under the rules of the former third pillar) the limited powers of the Court of Justice remain unchanged for a transition period of five years, unless the act is amended during that period.

- The **European Ombudsman** in Strasbourg investigates complaints about maladministration in the institutions and bodies of the EU. The ombudsman does not have legal powers, but can report non-compliance with its advice to the European Parliament.

3.7 Summary: Essential aspects of the EU's institutional set-up

As the initiator of legislation, the European Commission plays a central role as an agenda-setter in the European decision-making process. It is generally receptive to external recommendations and maintains close ties with national experts and policy-makers (at the EU and national levels) as well as with the various stakeholders potentially concerned by European legislation (see also chapter 10 on interest representation). The European Commission is always represented at meetings of the Council of Ministers and the European Commission President takes part in all meetings of the European Council. In the CFSP the European Commission plays a much more limited role.

Final decisions are generally taken by the Council of Ministers and the European Parliament, at least in the many areas where the ordinary legislative procedure (co-decision) applies (Figure 5). Where national vetoes have been abolished in the Council (i.e. where qualified majority voting applies), national governments are forced to reach real compromise. Negotiations continue to be dominated by a spirit of cooperation where preference is given to reaching a consensus that is acceptable to all delegations. In areas where unanimity is required (e.g. in the area of taxation), decisions tend to be based on the lowest common denominator, such that major steps towards European integration seldom take place. Most of the Council's work is accomplished by Council working groups (composed of national civil servants and diplomats) and within COREPER (the body bringing together EU ambassadors or deputy ambassadors). As it is familiar with the situation in both the member states and the Council, COREPER is usually well placed to judge what can realistically be achieved.

The European Parliament is the institution that has seen the greatest increase in competences with the successive treaty reforms. Under the ordinary legislative procedure it is an equal legislator to the member states in the Council. As the only EU institution directly elected by European citizens it enhances the democratic legitimacy of the

European decision-making process, but faces the challenge of a relatively low turnout in European elections.[66]

Other bodies such as the Committee of the Regions and the much older Economic and Social Committee are merely consultative but in certain cases can help to shape an agenda or influence the decision-making process.

Figure 5. The European institutions – Overview

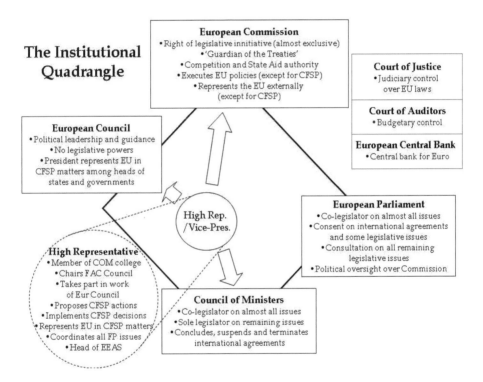

---

[66] Voter turnout at the European parliamentary elections has seen a steady decline from a high of 62% in the first direct elections for the European Parliament in 1979 (for the EU-9) to 50% in 1999 (EU-15) and 43% in 2009 (EU-27).

4.   How the EU legislates

Decision-making in the EU is highly complex. This is no different from national decision-making. One difference, however, is that EU decision-making has evolved considerably in line with progress on integration, thus underlining the EU's nature as an ever-changing Union. Established procedures are adapted quickly when a new treaty enters into force.[67]

This chapter does not go into detail about the formal procedures, as these are discussed in textbooks about European integration.[68] Instead it outlines the key features for understanding the basics. The chapter should be read in conjunction with the preceding chapter on the EU institutions, where the roles of the various institutions in the decision-making process are described in greater detail.

4.1   Legal acts of the Union

Legal acts of the EU can take different forms: regulations, directives, decisions, recommendations and opinions (Art. 288 TFEU).[69] While the first three are binding, recommendations and opinions do not have binding force.

---

[67] For example, when the Treaty of Lisbon entered into force, the European Commission published a Communication (Consequences of the entry into force of the Treaty of Lisbon for ongoing inter-institutional decision-making procedures, COM(2009) 665 final, Brussels, 2 December 2009) explaining its position on all pending legislative procedures. The proposals made under the rules of the third pillar were withdrawn. The European Parliament reacted with a resolution on 5 May 2010 demanding a new proposal on 10 additional files and announcing a new first reading concerning 4 procedures that had changed under the Treaty of Lisbon, while confirming its position on 29 procedures.

[68] See for instance, Bomberg et al. (2008), op. cit., (ch. 7); Dinan (2010), op. cit.; and Nugent (2010), op. cit.

[69] The Lisbon Treaty has abolished the specific instruments that were used in the third pillar covering police and judicial cooperation on criminal matters, which were called 'common positions', 'framework decisions' and 'conventions'.

The Treaty of Lisbon introduced a clear distinction between legislative acts on the one hand (i.e. acts to be adopted by the ordinary or a special legislative procedure, as explicitly indicated by the respective Treaty provision) and non-legislative acts on the other (Art. 289(3) TFEU). Legislative acts have to take the form of regulations, directives or decisions. Non-legislative acts can be legally binding (e.g. 'delegated acts' or 'implementing acts', see above subsection 3.3.2(iii)) or not (recommendations or opinions). In the area of CFSP, legislative acts are explicitly excluded (Art. 24(1), second subparagraph TEU). With the entry into force of the Treaty of Lisbon all acts adopted under CFSP are now called 'decisions' (Art. 25 TEU).[70]

The next two subsections outline the legal acts that exist under the Treaty of Lisbon.

4.1.1 Legislative acts

- **Regulations** are addressed to all member states and persons in the EU and are directly binding in their entirety, which would mean in principle that no national legislation is needed for implementation. Still, in practice national legislation frequently has to be changed or removed in order to comply with regulations.

- **Directives** are addressed to all or a specified number of member states. They normally just define the objectives and results to be achieved, and they require transposition into national law by a fixed date (e.g. two years). Failing this, recourse to the General Court or the Court of Justice is possible for reasons of non-implementation.

  Decisions are addressed to particular member states, companies or private individuals, and are binding upon those to whom they are addressed. Many are issued by the European Commission and typically concern cases of state aid and competition.

  Although there are more regulations and decisions in quantitative terms, directives tend to be considered the 'most important tools' as

---

[70] Decisions have replaced the previous set of instruments, which were called 'common strategies', 'joint actions' or 'common positions' (see ex-Art. 12 TEU).

they are often particularly significant in terms of impact. But this does not exclude that regulations and decisions can also have a high impact.

4.1.2 Non-legislative acts

- **Delegated acts** are legally binding acts that are adopted by the European Commission. They are acts of general application to supplement or amend certain non-essential elements of a legislative act. This legislative act (which is always required as a legal basis for the delegated act) must explicitly lay down the conditions to which the delegation is subject. A delegated act may only enter into force if neither the European Parliament nor the Council have objected to it; both institutions may also revoke the delegation to the European Commission altogether.

- **Implementing acts** are legally binding acts that confer implementing powers on the European Commission, or in specific cases on the Council, where uniform conditions for implementing legally binding Union acts are needed. The exercise of the European Commission's implementing powers is controlled by member states through the comitology committees (see subsection 3.3.2(iii)).

- **Recommendations and opinions** give non-binding views on a number of topics, normally to encourage desirable, but not legally enforceable, good practice throughout the Union.

  Communications, **White Papers** and **Green Papers** are not considered 'legal acts' according to the Treaties. The European Commission can issue them in all policy areas. They are non-binding but can have considerable influence since they help to formulate policy. Communications usually describe the status quo of a policy area with or without putting forward possible options. Green Papers usually launch a wide consultation process, while White Papers outline a more or less agreed policy and therefore make it easy to 'read' this policy. In reality, however, the boundaries between the three are often more blurred.

4.2 How acts are adopted

The main actors in the formal decision-making process are the Council of Ministers, the European Commission and the European Parliament. Until the Treaty of Maastricht the roles were clear: the European

Commission proposed, the European Parliament amended and the Council disposed (either by unanimity or by qualified majority, depending on the subject). Yet over time, the Parliament has obtained true co-decision power in a great number of areas. This means that instead of the traditional division with the Parliament amending and the Council disposing, both now jointly have to agree in most cases, if necessary in a conciliation procedure (as discussed below).[71] Procedures differ according to two criteria:

- the powers of the European Parliament, and
- the question of whether majority voting or unanimity is required in the Council.

4.2.1 Legislative procedures

The Treaties distinguish between the ordinary legislative procedure (co-decision) and various 'special legislative procedures'.

The point of departure is normally a legislative proposal from the European Commission that is then subject to approval, rejection or amendments either by both the European Parliament and the Council or – exceptionally – by the Council alone.

i) Ordinary legislative procedure

The European Parliament is strongest under the **ordinary legislative procedure**, as it grants Parliament powers equal to those of the Council (see Figure 6 and appendix 2). The procedure is essentially what was known as the 'co-decision procedure' before the Treaty of Lisbon. It is now the default (and therefore 'ordinary') legislative procedure of the EU and the only one explicitly outlined in the Treaty (Art. 294 TFEU). In the years before the Treaty of Lisbon, co-decision had already been the most important procedure, in terms of both its frequency of use and the significance of the decisions made. Co-decision was introduced by the Treaty of Maastricht and its field of application has been extended with every subsequent treaty reform (i.e. Amsterdam, Nice and Lisbon).

---

[71] See P.M. Kaczyński et al., *The Treaty of Lisbon: A Second Look at the Institutional Innovations*, Joint study by the Centre for European Policy Studies, Egmont and the European Policy Centre, Brussels, 2010.

Initially, it was feared that co-decision would make decision-making too complicated, but practice showed that the procedure worked well, although somewhat slowly during the first years. This prompted the member states to attach a protocol to the Amsterdam Treaty adjuring the Council, Commission and European Parliament to use this procedure as speedily as possible. As a result, many decisions are taken using an informal fast-track procedure with consultations between the Council and the Parliament reduced to one reading (instead of two or three) in practice (through 'trilogues'). Since 2004 a considerable increase in agreements reached during the first reading has been observed (from one-third to more than two-thirds of all legislation agreed under co-decision),[72] which has led to growing concern among MEPs about too many 'quick deal' agreements that may come at the disadvantage of the European Parliament.[73]

If the Council and European Parliament cannot agree during the first two readings, they have a last chance to do so in a conciliation committee, where selected representatives from the Council and the Parliament plus the European Commission try to reach agreement (although for the most part these actors convene at earlier stages of the process in the informal trilogues). If the conciliation committee reaches an agreement, the member states in the Council and the parliamentary plenary have to decide upon it. If no agreement is reached at that stage, then the legislative proposal has finally failed to be adopted (see appendix 2). This is not often the case, however. Of the eight legislative texts that were agreed in the conciliation committee in 2009, all have been approved subsequently by the Council and European Parliament in a third reading.[74]

---

[72] See the website of the European Commission, "Co-decision", "Statistics", 30 July 2010 (http://ec.europa.eu/codecision/statistics/index_en.htm).

[73] See S. Taylor, "MEPs quick-deal concerns: Deputies fear that co-decision deals with the Council could lead to poorer quality legislation", *European Voice*, 17-23 January 2008, p. 4.

[74] See website of the European Commission, "Co-decision", "Overview of Co-Decision Procedures Concluded on Conciliation" 30 July 2010 (http://ec.europa.eu/codecision/concluded/conciliation_en.htm).

Figure 6. Schematic overview of the ordinary legislative procedure

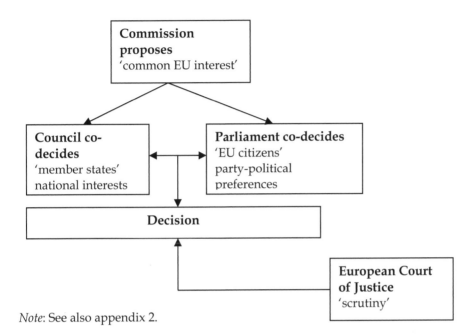

Note: See also appendix 2.

ii) *Special legislative procedures*

There are several special legislative procedures that are not explicitly outlined in the Treaties.[75]

- The **consent procedure** gives the European Parliament a right to accept or reject a particular proposal. It covers only a small number of legislative areas, such as combating discrimination (Art. 19(1) TFEU), extending citizenship-related rights (Art. 25

---

[75] Art. 289(2) TFEU only refers to them as procedures for the adoption of a legislative act by the Council with the participation of the European Parliament, and by the European Parliament with the participation of the Council.

Note that the cooperation procedure (ex-Art. 252 TEC) has been abolished with the Treaty of Lisbon. Under the Treaty of Nice it was only applied to very few cases in the field of Economic and Monetary Union.

TFEU) and adopting the multi-annual financial framework (Art. 312(2) TFEU). The Council acts unanimously in all of these cases.[76]

The consent of the European Parliament is often also required in the context of *non-legislative* procedures, such as EU enlargement (e.g. adhesion treaties for new member states) and association or trade agreements with non-EU countries. The Treaty of Lisbon has extended the requirement of the European Parliament's consent to the conclusion of most international agreements.[77]

- The European Parliament is weakest under the **consultation procedure**,[78] which merely requires its non-binding opinion.[79] Although its rights in areas falling under this procedure are very limited, it still has the (political) possibility to link them to areas falling under the ordinary legislative procedure or to its budgetary powers. Without the European Parliament's agreement, there is no budget, and it has used this power in the past to extend its influence in other areas.

---

[76] The only case where the Council acts by qualified majority in the context of a *legislative* procedure and where the European Parliament has to give its consent, concerns implementing measures of the Union's own resources system (Art. 311, para. 4 TFEU).

[77] See Art. 218(6)(v) TFEU, which stipulates that agreements require the European Parliament's consent if they cover policy fields to which either the ordinary legislative procedure or the consent procedure applies. This means that notably all trade agreements require the European Parliament's consent.

[78] When a legislative procedure requires consultation of the European Parliament, the Council normally acts unanimously. In the framework of a legislative procedure there are only three cases for which the Council acts with qualified majority when the European Parliament is consulted:

- measures to facilitate diplomatic protection (Art. 23 TFEU);
- research, i.e. specific programmes implementing the framework programme (Art. 182(4) TFEU); and
- measures concerning the outermost regions (Art. 349 TFEU).

[79] Still, according to an ECJ ruling (in the 'Isoglucose' Case 138/79, *Roquette Frères v. Council* [1980] ECR 3333) "due consultation" of the European Parliament constitutes an essential formality. Disregard of this formality means that the measure concerned is invalid.

4.2.2 Non-legislative procedures

Some legally binding acts are adopted through a non-legislative procedure. Such a procedure can involve both the Council of Ministers and the European Commission (e.g. a common customs tariff, Art. 31 TFEU), the Commission alone (e.g. undertakings with a special position, Art. 106(3) TFEU) or the Commission, social partners and the Council (agreements in the area of social policy, Arts 154 and 155 TFEU).

Delegated and implementing acts are also legally binding acts that are adopted according to non-legislative procedures. The same is true for the conclusion of international agreements (see the discussion in subsection 4.2.1(ii) above).

5. What is the difference between the EU and a federal state?

The EU is often wrongly compared with a classic federation like the US, Germany or Switzerland. Federations tend to have a separation of powers among the different levels of government and a clear distinction of the competences of the various institutional actors. Neither is true for the EU, however, where *power is dispersed* across the institutions. The European Commission, the member states and the European Parliament must interact as partners in drafting, adopting, implementing and enforcing legislation. Although the European Commission has the right of initiative, it consults closely with member states and (where the ordinary legislative procedure applies) with the European Parliament when drafting legislation. During the decision-making phase the European Commission participates in the deliberations and negotiations among member states. While it does not have a vote, the European Commission still plays a crucial role at this stage. And although the Parliament will only formally decide after the Council has taken its decision, the Parliament will have already been consulted informally. Once the decision has been adopted (by the Council and Parliament), member states and the European Commission must jointly implement the decision. With delegated acts the European Commission can supplement or amend non-essential elements of a legislative act (see section 3.3.2(iii)), but the Parliament and the Council both have a right to veto such an act or even revoke the delegation altogether. In addition, given its extended powers in many areas, confrontation with the European Parliament in an area where it does not have formal powers can still backfire for the Council or the European Commission in another area where the Parliament does have such power (e.g. on budgetary aspects). Thus, in reality at every level and in every phase of the decision-making process, the powers of the European Commission, member states and the European Parliament are mixed. At times national governments present themselves as being in opposition to the EU, but they are just as much a part of the EU decision-making process as the European Commission and the European Parliament.

Another feature that distinguishes the EU from most (federal) states is its strong focus on consensus building and the avoidance of decisions based on simple majorities. The EU decision-making process usually requires large coalitions. Majorities are not stable (i.e. no 'government vs. opposition') as they shift from issue to issue. The decision-making process is based on power sharing between institutions and requires mutual trust among the actors. For example, in the Council, a sense of constructive cooperation usually prevails over power struggles among countries and the concerns of smaller member states are traditionally respected. The wider public sometimes perceives the EU decision-making process as opaque, slow and seemingly inefficient, but it produces lasting decisions that are acceptable in a diverse range of national contexts. This process additionally enhances the prospects for coherent implementation across the EU.

6. Does the EU suffer from a 'democratic deficit' and does the Treaty of Lisbon make the EU more democratic?

For many years there has been a controversial debate, in both academic circles and in the wider public, on whether the EU has sufficient democratic legitimacy for its often far-reaching decisions.[80] Owing to the Union's distinct *sui generis* character, it is not easy (nor sensible) to apply the same standards and mechanisms that apply to a nation state on the one hand or to a traditional international organisation on the other. The EU has considerably more powers than most international organisations (e.g. the European Commission's (sole) right of initiative in its areas of

---

[80] See also S. Hix, *What's wrong with the European Union and how to fix it*, 1st edition, Cambridge, UK and Malden, MA: Polity Press, 2008.

competence or the abolition of national vetoes in the Council on many policy issues), but it also has considerably fewer powers than a nation state (e.g. no competences to attribute itself competences, to raise taxes or to direct an army). In addition, the EU has to act in a context where it cannot count on a common public forum, as the national level remains predominant with respect to media attention and citizens' identity. It is therefore difficult to envisage enhancing the EU's legitimacy with the introduction of a majoritarian system as known in most member states. The complex political context of the EU is therefore reflected in its entire decision-making system: at the beginning of a legislative procedure is a proposal from the European Commission, and thus it arises from the institution that is best placed to represent the general 'Union interest' and not a specific national or party-political preference. Decisions in the Council are in practice often taken by consensus and even in the case of a vote, not just a simple but rather a qualified majority must be reached. This qualified majority is calculated according to a double-majority system, which again reflects the particular respect for minority positions. In the European Parliament the allocation of seats is digressively proportionate to the size of the country from which representatives originate in order to guarantee that citizens from the smallest countries have a meaningful number of deputies.

The Treaty of Lisbon has not put into question this *sui generis* character of the Union, but departing from this assumption, it has enhanced the democratic legitimacy of the Union in a number of ways:

- The Treaty explicitly stresses the **values** of the EU, which for example provide guidance to the legislative proposals of the European Commission or the rulings of the European Court of Justice. As such, the Treaty states that the Union is founded on the respect for human dignity, freedom, democracy, equality, the rule of law and respect for human rights (Art. 2 TEU).

- The Treaty of Lisbon has also introduced a **separate title on "Democratic Principles"** that regroups and highlights all respective provisions. Notably it states that every citizen shall have the right to participate in the democratic life of the Union and that decisions shall be taken as openly and as closely as possible to citizens.

- Besides these horizontal provisions, the Treaty strengthens democracy at three levels:

    - at the EU level by giving the European Parliament more competences,

    - at the member state level by strengthening control of national parliaments, and

    - directly at the citizens' level through the introduction of the European Citizens' Initiative and through the Charter of Fundamental Rights becoming legally binding.

- As concerns the **European Parliament**, the only directly elected EU institution has become an equal co-legislator to the national ministers in the Council on almost all policy areas (e.g. newly including large parts of agricultural policy, trade policy and the area of freedom, security and justice). Additionally, the approval of the Parliament is now needed for all international treaties that cover matters falling under the ordinary legislative procedure or the consent procedure (which is one of the special legislative procedures, see above 4.2.1 (ii)). It has increased budgetary powers for the annual budget, giving the European Parliament the final word on all categories of spending. Following the parliamentary elections, the European Parliament formally elects the President of the European Commission. A direct link between the outcome of the parliamentary elections and the President of the EU's main executive body is thus established. Finally, the European Parliament is likely to play a greater role during future treaty revisions. Most importantly, it may submit proposals for the amendment of the Treaties to the Council. Before the Treaty of Lisbon, only national governments or the European Commission were entitled to do so.

- As **national parliaments** remain the focal points for political debate in the member states, they are of key importance to stimulate discussion on European issues and foster a better understanding of EU decisions in national publics. The Treaty of Lisbon has introduced a new article (Art. 12 TEU) that sets out their rights and functions in relation to the Union, covering for example the information they receive, the review of the subsidiarity principle, evaluation mechanisms in the area of freedom, security and justice as well as the revision of the Treaties. Maybe most importantly, the Protocol on the Application of the Principles of Subsidiarity and Proportionality has been amended to allow closer scrutiny of the subsidiarity principle by national parliaments.[81] Any national parliament can also block a unanimous decision by member states intended to shift decision-making from the unanimity rule to qualified majority voting (so-called 'passerelle clauses').[82] Finally yet importantly, national parliaments are set to play an even greater role during future treaty reforms. While before they were already central actors during the ratification phase, the Treaty of Lisbon has introduced

---

[81] Under this 'early-warning system', any national parliament may, within eight weeks of the last language version of a legislative proposal being ready, issue a reasoned opinion stating why it considers that the proposal does not comply with the principle of subsidiarity.

- If the reasoned opinion represents at least one-third of the votes allocated to national parliaments, the author of the proposal (primarily the European Commission) must review the text. Following this review, the author may decide to maintain, amend or withdraw the draft. Reasons must be given for this decision ('yellow card').

- If, under the ordinary legislative procedure (co-decision), the legislative proposal is challenged by a simple majority of the votes allocated to national parliaments and if the European Commission decides to maintain its proposal regardless, a *special procedure* comes into play. The European Commission has to issue a reasoned opinion explaining how the principle of subsidiarity is being respected. This opinion is sent to the legislator (the Council and European Parliament), together with the reasoned opinions of the national parliaments. The legislator may then decide (by 55% of the members of the Council or by a majority of the votes cast in the European Parliament) not to continue with the legislative procedure. This mechanism ensures closer scrutiny of the subsidiarity principle without, however, undermining the European Commission's right of initiative ('orange card').

[82] National parliaments can veto such a move in the area of family law with cross-border implications (e.g. legislation on bi-national marriages) or some future treaty revisions (but only the 'ordinary' revisions and not the 'simplified' smaller treaty changes, which do not increase the powers allocated to the Union and are limited to Part III TFEU on internal policies).

a convention as part of the ordinary treaty revision procedure. In such a convention national parliaments will be represented, as was the case for the Convention on the Future of Europe in 2002–03.

- For the first time, the EU Treaties also include an instrument of direct democracy: the **European Citizens' Initiative,** giving one million citizens from one quarter of the member states (i.e. currently seven)[83] the possibility to 'invite' the European Commission to make a legislative proposal on issues that fall within the remit of its competence to implement the Treaties (e.g. consumer protection, environmental standards or working conditions). The ultimate decision to make a proposal remains with the European Commission, but it will justify itself with a Communication if it decides not to take action. The European Citizens' Initiative is less of a legal instrument than a tool to increase political debate and pressure for action.

- Finally there are two other innovations that enhance citizens' rights vis-à-vis EU institutions: the fact that the Charter of Fundamental Rights has become legally binding and the foreseen accession of the EU to the European Convention on Human Rights (ECHR).

  – The Charter of Fundamental Rights sets out in a single text the full range of civil, political, economic and social rights of European citizens and all persons resident in the EU. A first version had already been adopted in 2000, but it had only a declaratory character. The Charter is not an integral part of the Treaty of Lisbon, but the Treaty contains a reference to the Charter, which makes it legally binding. This means that the Charter has to be observed by all institutions and bodies of the EU as well as by member states when they are

---

[83] The Treaty (Art. 11 TEU) requires "a significant number of Member States", which has been determined as one quarter in the regulation establishing the procedures and conditions required for a citizens' initiative. The regulation was signed on 16 February 2011 by the Council and Parliament. Member states now have 12 months to adjust their national regulations, so that the first collection of signatures can start in March 2012.

implementing EU law. Its provisions shall not extend in any way the competences of the Union as defined in the Treaties, however (Art. 6(1) TEU).

— The Treaty of Lisbon has also introduced a new legal basis that allows for the accession of the EU to the ECHR, to which all member states are already party. When the EU accedes to the ECHR, the European Court of Human Rights in Strasbourg will be able to scrutinise compliance of the EU's acts with the Convention. Accession will additionally provide a new possibility for legal remedies for individuals.[84]

The challenge of how to close the gap between the EU institutions and citizens remains and it may even become one of the dominant questions for the Union's future. The Treaty of Lisbon in itself does not solve the problem alone, yet it offers a number of instruments that improve on the situation.

7. Key concepts and principles of the EU

The Treaty on European Union contains two provisions highlighting the values (Art. 2 TEU)[85] and objectives (Art. 3 TEU)[86] of the Union. They

---

[84] Accession negotiations between the EU and the Council of Europe started on 7 July 2010.

[85] The values are respect for human dignity, freedom, democracy, equality, the rule of law and respect for human rights, including the rights of persons belonging to minorities. Art. 2 TEU (as revised by the Treaty of Lisbon) states that these values are common to the member states in a society in which pluralism, non-discrimination, tolerance, justice, solidarity and equality between men and women prevail.

[86] The objectives of the Union mentioned in Art. 3 TEU are more numerous and broader in scope than those listed in ex-Art. 2 TEU (i.e. before the Treaty of Lisbon). Art. 3 TEU includes for example peace, full employment, sustainable development, cultural diversity, solidarity, cohesion and protection of citizens. By contrast, the principle of "free and undistorted competition" already set out in ex-Arts. 3 and 4 of the EC Treaty, is not mentioned among the objectives of the Union, as competition is not an end in itself. This does not affect the scope or specific weight of the competition rules, however, as they are highlighted in

guide the EU institutions when legislating and implementing EU law, as well as the European Court of Justice when it issues rulings. The values of the Union also constitute the reference framework for future accessions to the Union, and for any sanctions on member states that infringe those values in a serious and persistent manner (Art. 7 TEU).

At the same time, the following list – mostly relating to the traditional, economic integration objectives – goes beyond these two articles. The EU as a highly decentralised and emerging political system is founded on a number of key concepts and principles. Taking a closer look at them should allow a better understanding of the EU's essence.[87]

- The *principle of sincere cooperation* (Art. 4(3) TEU) commits the member states and the Union to assisting each other in carrying out the tasks resulting from the Treaties. This is particularly important given the high level of decentralisation in the EU (see chapter 5). Consequently, if member states (in the Council) fail to act, Art. 265 TFEU offers the possibility to bring an action before the European Court of Justice, an instrument that has been used very successfully in the past. The principle of sincere cooperation is further reflected in the implementation of Union law. Although the European Commission and the Court have the right to control implementation and enforcement, without full cooperation of the member states the EU legal system could not function.

- *Non-discrimination as to nationality* (Art. 18 TFEU) ties the hands of member states in promoting national solutions that would come at the expense of other member states. The application of this principle has been enforced by a constant review of national legislation as to potential restrictions for other EU nationals. This has resulted in ensuring the free movement of goods and services and the right of establishment. EU citizens are free to choose where they want to live and work.

---

the new Protocol on the Internal Market and Competition (which has the same legal value as the Treaties).

[87] Most principles are discussed in greater detail in J. Pelkmans, *European Integration – Methods and Economic Analysis*, 3rd edition, Pearson Education, 2006, pp. 24-25.

- The *principle of conferral* (Art. 5(2) TEU) determines that the Union shall only act within the limits of the competences conferred upon it by the member states. Competences that are not explicitly agreed in the Treaties by all member states remain in the national domain. The EU thus has no competence to attribute itself additional competences (referred to as *'Kompetenz-Kompetenz'*). Art. 352 TFEU provides a legal base for new competences, however, if member states agree unanimously and "if action by the Union should prove necessary to attain one of the objectives set out in the Treaties, and the Treaties have not provided the necessary powers". Notably, measures in the area of CFSP are explicitly excluded in Art. 352(4) TFEU.

- The *subsidiarity* and *proportionality principles* (Arts 5(3) and (4) TEU)[88] deal with the proper exercise of EU competences or authority. Both are used to identify the proper level of government in a multi-tier system. According to this principle an issue should only be tackled at the EU level if it cannot be done just as effectively at the national level. The principle of proportionality demands that all measures taken by the EU be proportionate to reaching the aims of the Treaties.

A general guiding principle is the respect of the *acquis communautaire*, as the EU is a union based on law. The *acquis* includes the complete body of EU legislation, including secondary and case law. All the member states have to comply with it, unless they have

---

[88] Art. 5(3) TEU states,

> [u]nder the principle of subsidiarity, in areas which do not fall within its exclusive competence, the Union shall act only if and in so far as the objectives of the proposed action cannot be sufficiently achieved by the Member States, either at central level or at regional and local level, but can rather, by reason of the scale of effects of the proposed action, be better achieved at Union level.

Art. 5(4) TEU states,

> [u]nder the principle of proportionality, the content and form of Union action shall not exceed what is necessary to achieve the objectives of the Treaties.

negotiated an opt-out.[89] The notion of the *acquis communautaire* is particularly important in the context of EU enlargement, as new members have to accept the full *acquis*. Although new members might get transition periods for implementation, they will not be granted permanent opt-outs (e.g. like the UK and Denmark regarding the single currency).

8.   The EU budget

'Rules, not money' is an implicit principle defining the EU as a regulatory body and not a big spender. Government functions that typically require large resources (social benefits, defence, education or pensions) have remained in national hands (see also chapter 9 on the euro). If the EU engages in policy areas through common policies, its involvement is mainly in the regulatory field. Only in the fields of agriculture and regional policy (structural funds and the cohesion fund) can resources be termed substantial. For the 2007–13 period, agriculture and structural funds made up nearly 70% of the total budget, almost equally shared between the two.[90]

The high shares allocated to agriculture and regional policy can partly be explained by equity considerations. Agricultural spending addresses – among other issues – income discrepancies within the sector while the structural funds address those between nations, which have emerged with subsequent enlargements. Finally, in the past the structure of the EU's budget was influenced by the need to ensure that all member states agree on two fundamental EU objectives: the internal market and monetary union. Historically the compensatory aspect of the EU budget is perhaps best understood if placed in the context of negotiations on a multilateral agreement.[91]

---

[89] An 'opt-out' refers to a member state having negotiated for a particular treaty provision(s) to not apply to it.

[90] Agricultural policy falls under budget heading 2, "preservation and management of natural resources", from which around 9% has to be subtracted for rural development.

[91] The net balance disputes emerging with great regularity throughout each negotiation cycle fit best into game theory models on political power. See H.

The annual EU budget falls within a longer-term financial framework jointly agreed by the European Commission, the European Parliament and the Council of Ministers. The current agreement covers the period 2007–13 (see Figure 7). The multi-annual framework under the new Treaty will take the form of a Council regulation to which the European Parliament has to give its consent (Art. 312 TFEU). It will set concrete ceilings for the categories of expenditure mentioned.

Figure 7. EU budget composition, Financial Perspectives for 2007–13

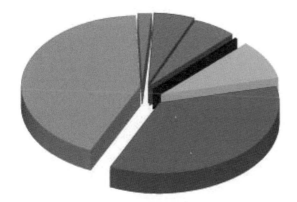

- 1a. Competitiveness for growth and employment : 9 %
- 1b. Cohesion for growth and employment : 35,6 %
- 2. Preservation and management of natural resources : 42,5 %
- 3   a. Freedom, security and justice : 0,8 %
      b. Citizenship : 0,5 %
- 4. The EU as a global player (excl. EDF) : 5,7 %
- 5. Total administrative expenditure : 5,8 %
- 6. Compensations BG/RO : 0,1 %

Source: European Commission website, "Financial Programming and Budget", "Financial Framework for the enlarged Union (2007-2013)" (http://ec.europa.eu/budget/prior_future/fin_framework_en.htm).

Kauppi and W. Widgrén, *Voting rules and budget allocation in an enlarged EU,* CEPR Discussion Paper No. 5134, Centre for Economic and Policy Research, London, 2006.

Following the new budgetary procedure of the Treaty of Lisbon the European Parliament has a say on all categories of spending in the annual budget. The procedure resembles the ordinary (co-decision) procedure, with one reading followed by conciliation (Art. 314 TFEU).

As for the EU as a whole, there are some ground rules for the budget. *Subsidiarity* also applies to the budget: the EU should only act and spend if it is better suited to do so, compared with lower levels of governance. Inextricably linked to subsidiarity is the *proportionality* principle, i.e. the content and form of EU action should not exceed what is necessary to achieve the objective. Moreover, EU money should neither substitute for national funding, nor should EU funding reduce aggregate national public spending. This is described as *additionality*.

Therefore, the EU budget is by no means comparable to national budgets, for which figures range between 40% and 50% of GDP. The 2010 EU budget comprised €141.4 billion in commitment appropriations, which was less than the agreed ceiling of 1.24% of total EU GDP.[92]

The biggest share of the 2010 budget was spent on "sustainable growth" (45.4%) and included both cohesion (34.9%) and competitiveness (14.9%). Cohesion is primarily addressed by the structural funds and the cohesion fund, which are the financial instruments of the EU's regional policy to narrow the development disparities among regions and member states. The largest share of the funds allocated under the competitiveness heading are spent on EU research and development programmes. Through these programmes, the EU has become a large funder of fundamental and applied research (see Box 6).

---

[92] Derived from the Financial Programming and Budget website of the European Commission, "Where does the money come from?" (http://ec.europa.eu/budget/budget_glance/where_from_en.htm). For further information, see also on the same website, "The current year: 2010 – investing to restore jobs and growth" (http://ec.europa.eu/budget/budget_detail/current_year_en.htm).

Box 6. EU R&D spending – A relatively new priority

The idea of using EU funding (e.g. the EU budget or the European Investment Bank) to contribute significantly to research and development (R&D) in Europe is rather novel. Originally, research spending was concentrated on specific sectors originating from the Coal and Steel and Euratom Treaties. On energy, finance was limited to the objectives of Euratom. R&D as a public policy at the EU level for promoting growth was not a major issue prior to the Lisbon Strategy for Growth and Jobs in 2000. Additional momentum has gradually been building in the context of the global climate change negotiations, where technology has moved to the top of the agenda.

For the Financial Perspectives period of 2007–13, the funding for the Seventh Framework Programme (FP7) is €53.2 billion, representing a very significant increase from the previous period.

The central funding mechanism at the EU level for research and innovation comes through the framework programmes. The first one originated in 1984 and currently we are at the seventh. Today's FP7 is providing a particularly important turning point: the EU's research strategy is based on advancing the European Research Area initiative, which focuses on increasing the number of scientists, the level of private and public research funding (aimed at reaching 3% of the EU's GDP) and the quality of research in Europe, taking advantage of the economies of scale created by cross-border cooperation. In addition, the EU has set up the European Research Council (ERC), which concentrates on funding frontier research, and a number of agencies to better manage the programmes while leaving the European Commission and the ERC to concentrate on policy and research excellence rather than procedures. To this, one has to add the creation of the European Institute of Innovation and Technology and its 'Knowledge and Innovation Communities', for highly integrated partnerships for bundling European excellence.

Specifically on energy – as a key technology component of climate change – the EU has developed and approved a Strategic Energy Technology Plan, a technology roadmap with a very detailed description until 2020 of the financial requirements and the areas of research involved.

The next largest item is "preservation and management of natural resources" (agricultural expenditure and rural development), which accounts for 42% of the total budget (31% for agricultural expenditure), disbursed through several different instruments. Other areas are external relations (the "EU as a global player"), which accounts for 5.7%, and "citizenship, freedom, security and justice" (1.2%). The amount spent on administration is 5.6%. Two additional expenditures fall outside the official EU budget: the European development fund (EDF), with €22.7 billion in the period 2008–13; and military operations, which are decided upon through the ad-hoc 'Athena' mechanism. Concerning the EDF, the Treaty of Lisbon has made it easier to envisage a future inclusion of the fund in the general budget ('budgetisation').

The EU has its own resources to finance its expenditure. Legally, these resources belong to the Union. Member states collect them on behalf of the EU and transfer them to the EU budget. There are three kinds of own resources:

- The *resource based on gross national income (GNI)* is a uniform percentage rate (0.73%) applied to the GNI of each member state (accounting for approximately 76% of total revenue).

- The *resource based on value added tax (VAT)* is a uniform percentage rate that is applied to each member state's harmonised VAT revenue (approximately 11% of total revenue).

- *Traditional own resources* mainly consist of duties charged on imports of products coming from a non-EU state (approximately 12% of total revenue).

The budget also receives *other revenues*, such as taxes paid by EU staff on their salaries, contributions from non-EU countries to certain EU programmes and fines on companies that breach competition or other laws (about 1% of total revenue).

9. The euro and its governance

Since the launch of the euro notes in January 2002, the 12-nation eurozone has steadily expanded to 17 members with the recent entry of Estonia. The UK and Denmark have retained a legal opt-out while all other member states (including those from Central and Eastern

Europe) that joined the EU after 2004 are legally obliged to adopt the euro once they fulfil the entry criteria, but they can of course choose not to fulfil the criteria.[93] Today the euro is the currency of some 330 million Europeans. In addition, it is also used in some microstates and is widely circulated in Eastern Europe and a number of former colonies of EU member states.

9.1   Governance

A common currency had long been an aspiration of advocates of European integration. Back in 1969 the heads of state and government of the then European Community agreed on a plan for Economic and Monetary Union, the Werner Plan. But it was never implemented and soon abandoned. Most of the member states of the subsequent European Economic Community agreed in 1972, after the demise of the Bretton Woods system of fixed exchange rates, to maintain stable exchange rates by preventing exchange rate fluctuations of more than 2.25% (termed the European 'currency snake') relative to each other. In 1979 the system was replaced by the European monetary system (EMS), which in theory was based on a new entity, the European Currency Unit (ECU) (a basket of currencies. In reality, however, the EMS was based on the Deutschemark and the German central bank (Deutsche Bundesbank) was at its centre. Because of the relative strength of the Deutschemark, and the low-inflation policies of the Bundesbank, all other currencies were de facto forced to follow its lead. The EMS was widely considered a 'disinflationary device', i.e. a mechanism that forced other member countries to converge gradually to German levels of inflation. It worked as long as other member countries had capital controls and thus could protect their exchange rates against large capital flows. Yet when capital markets were liberalised in the context of the internal market or EC 1992 programme (see also chapter 2), member states had to choose between potentially unstable exchange rates driven by destabilising speculation or a jump ahead to monetary union.

---

[93] Sweden is legally obliged to adopt the euro, but has not done so yet. A referendum in September 2003 saw 56.1% vote against membership in the eurozone.

As a result, the Treaty of Maastricht in 1992 established Economic and Monetary Union (EMU) as a formal objective, including the conditions that member states need to meet in order to join the euro. These conditions are known as 'convergence criteria'.[94] They are basically low and stable inflation, exchange rate stability and, critically, sound public finances, expressed as ceilings for budget deficits (3%) and debt per GDP (60%).

Responsibility for monetary policy lies with an independent institution, the European System of Central Banks, which comprises the ECB in Frankfurt and the central banks of the EU states that have joined the eurozone. Fiscal policy – taxes and expenditures – remain the sole responsibility of member states even in the EMU. The autonomy of member states is nonetheless constrained by common rules on public finances detailed in the Stability and Growth Pact (SGP), whose purpose is to ensure adherence to the fiscal stability criteria. Member states retain full responsibility for their own structural policies (i.e. labour, pension and capital markets) although they agree, at least on paper, to coordinate to reach the ultimate goals of stability, growth and employment. In the 1990s this set-up was considered sufficient to ensure the stability of the eurozone. Large fiscal transfers among member states or between the EU and member states were ruled out by the Maastricht Treaty (the no-bailout clause, now Art. 125 TFEU).

The SGP had already been agreed in 1996 to enforce observance of the fiscal convergence criteria. That notwithstanding, when Germany and France faced problems in observing the 3% deficit limit in 2003 they decided not to apply the strictures of the SGP and pushed instead for a Pact revision, which came into force in 2005. At the heart of the SGP is the excessive deficit procedure, which kicks in if member states fail to meet the Pact agreements, notably on public deficits and public debt. While the initial version of the SGP saw a quasi-automatic execution, the 2005 version became more flexible to accommodate different circumstances, especially the business cycle. The two national thresholds – 60% for debt and 3% for the deficit – remained unchanged,

---

[94] They are sometimes also called the 'Maastricht criteria'.

but in 2005 more flexibility and (to an extent) political discretion was introduced in the management of this excessive debt procedure.

The eurozone is represented politically by its finance ministers, known collectively as the Eurogroup – the meeting of the euro-area finance ministers that is currently presided by Luxembourg's Prime Minister Jean-Claude Juncker. This group usually meets a day before a meeting of the full Ecofin Council of all 27 member states. The Eurogroup is not an official Council formation but is mentioned in the Lisbon Treaty (Protocol No. 14) and when the full Ecofin Council votes on matters exclusively affecting the eurozone, only Eurogroup members are permitted to participate in the vote.

The establishment of the EMU has not changed the fact that only member states are full members of international financial institutions like the International Monetary Fund (IMF). The President of the ECB and the Eurogroup attend global fora such as the G-7, G-8 and G-20, but decisions are taken solely by representatives of member states.

9.2 Testing the euro: From the financial to the sovereign debt crisis

The financial crisis broke out in 2007–08 when banking systems around the globe were threatening to melt down in the aftermath of the bankruptcy of the US investment bank Lehman Brothers. The leaders of the euro area countries met for an emergency session in Paris and put together a huge package of national support measures for the banking system in the form of loan guarantees and capital for particularly weak banks. This package, whose headline figure was around €2 trillion, did indeed stop the panic and markets stabilised after a few turbulent months.

Still, euro governance was only put to a real test starting in spring 2010 when rising government deficits and debt levels in some peripheral euro-member countries created alarm in financial markets about a possible sovereign debt crisis. The crisis started with Greece (a member of the euro area since 2001), when it became apparent that the country had misstated its public deficit for some time, leading to Greece being frozen out of the financial markets in early 2010.

Yet Greece was not an isolated case. Debt from other countries, sometimes referred to as 'PIIGS' (Portugal, Italy, Ireland, Greece and

Spain), was also downgraded and the euro dropped in the foreign exchange markets as financial markets judged euro governance as inadequate.

There were no clear rules for how to deal with the financing difficulties of a euro area government as the situation was not supposed to arise. At the same time, financial markets within the eurozone have become so integrated that a sovereign default could lead to a generalised meltdown of financial markets, as occurred after the bankruptcy of Lehman Brothers in 2008. Indeed, this is what seemed to be starting in early May 2010 when there was not only a generalised sell of peripheral euro-area debt, but also signs of strains in many other, unrelated financial markets – not just in Europe. When faced with this danger of a widespread, financial market meltdown, the leaders of the eurozone met for a dramatic weekend summit in Brussels and put together a stabilisation package for the euro. The package consisted of a European Financial Stability Facility (EFSF), which could support euro area governments by raising up to €440 in funds.[95] Another €60 billion was found in nooks and crannies of the EU budget, bringing the package to €500 billion. The European Council also pressed the IMF into the game, pencilling in another €250 billion to bring the headline figure for the entire package up to €750 billion.

The creation of the EFSF at first seemed to calm the financial markets. At the end of October, however, turmoil erupted again when the extent of the losses in the Irish banking system became apparent and financial markets took fright at the suggestion of the German government that the private sector should somehow contribute to further rescues. The EFSF had clearly been seen as a temporary stopgap in Germany, which then insisted on a wider debate about the future of economic governance in the EU.

---

[95] As Germany did not want to create another institution, the EFSF operates for the time being through a nominally private 'special purpose vehicle' incorporated in Luxembourg.

9.3 Institutional adaptation following the crisis

The Greek crisis triggered reflection on how to strengthen and streamline economic governance of the eurozone to avoid a similar situation in the future. An initial result of this was the creation of a task force composed of finance ministers and headed by President of the European Council Herman Van Rompuy. In the autumn of 2010 this task force published a number of recommendations for strengthening the excessive deficit procedure of the Pact and also recommended the creation of a new 'excessive imbalances procedure' to allow the EU to address the problems instigated by countries running large deficits. At almost the same time the European Commission published very similar proposals (as part of its economic governance package),[96] which additionally included the idea of introducing 'reverse majority' provisions in the Pact. Under such provisions, proposals by the European Commission to countries with excessive deficits are to be considered automatically adopted unless the Council of Ministers overrules them with a qualified majority.

These proposals are likely to be adopted in 2011, as there is a consensus among all institutions – the European Commission, European Parliament, Council and the European Central Bank – on the need for broader and more effective surveillance of member states' fiscal as well as macroeconomic policies and structural reforms.

Another innovation that still needs to be fully implemented is a permanent crisis-resolution mechanism, i.e. a permanent EFSF. The European Council decided in October 2010 to start the process for a limited treaty amendment with the aim that any change could be ratified at the latest by mid-2013. It proposed to amend Art. 136 TFEU by introducing a new paragraph 3: "The Member States whose currency is the euro may establish a stability mechanism to be activated if indispensable to safeguard the stability of the euro area as a whole. The

---

[96] For more information, see the European Commission's website, "A new EU economic governance – A comprehensive Commission package of proposals", 29.9.2010 (http://ec.europa.eu/economy_finance/articles/eu_economic_situation/2010-09-eu_economic_governance_proposals_en.htm).

granting of any required financial assistance under the mechanism will be made subject to strict conditionality."

On 15 February 2011 the European Commission gave a positive opinion, stressing that the proposed amendment to the Treaty does not increase or dilute the competences of the Union. Following opinions of the European Parliament and the ECB, the heads of state and government formally agreed on the Treaty amendment at the European Council meeting of 24 March 2011. The so-called 'simplified revision procedure' (introduced by the Lisbon Treaty) will be sufficient for the limited change.

Although the creation of the permanent crisis-resolution mechanism has attracted most attention, other reforms might turn out to be at least as important. One key issue here is the supervision of banking in the EU. Supervision of the financial service industry has remained in the hands of member states, although there is an EU-wide internal market for financial services, where financial service companies operate across borders. Until 2010 the coordination of regulation was undertaken by three separate committees on banking, insurance and securities, with few real powers. This has changed in 2011 with the creation of three agencies to oversee financial stability for banking (the European Banking Authority (EBA)), insurance and occupational pensions (the European Insurance and Occupational Pensions Authority (EIOPA)) and securities markets (European Securities and Markets Authority (ESMA)), leading to a new financial supervisory framework in Europe. The agencies are responsible for drafting harmonised technical standards and mediating in the event of disputes between national regulators. The new authorities have no direct supervisory powers, other than for credit-rating agencies operating in the EU. They can acquire EU-wide supervisory powers, however, should member states decide that an 'emergency' situation exists. Day-to-day oversight of individual companies and markets remains the task of national supervisory agencies. The seats of the new authorities are divided between London (EBA), Paris (ESMA) and Frankfurt (EIOPA).

Another step forward comes with the establishment of the European Systemic Risk Board, whose task is to assess threats to financial stability in general. This new body, managed de facto by the ECB, might also play an important role in the evolving economic governance of the euro area.

10.   Lobbying and interest representation

The fact that much economic regulation emanates from the EU level has made Brussels an important place where interest groups attempt to inform and influence the policy-making process. Since the 1980s the successive expansions of EU competences and increase in the powers of the European Parliament have led to a gradual growth of advocacy and lobby groups. No definitive figures exist but the literature typically assumes some 15,000 lobbyists are practising their trade in Brussels.[97] They include private and public sector interests as diverse as businesses, their trade and professional associations and industry groupings, chambers of commerce, trade unions, regions, regional and local governments, churches and their organisations, non-government organisations (NGOs), non-profit organisations and think tanks. Also represented are international organisations, such as UN organisations or the World Bank, and finally public relations consultancies and law firms. In addition, the permanent representations of the EU member states and well over 100 diplomatic missions are attempting to defend their interests. We can assume that the vast majority of these groupings concentrate on collecting, processing and dispatching information and intelligence to keep their headquarters up to date with EU developments.

More and more interest groups, NGOs and think tanks seek to influence decisions from a European rather than just a national perspective. At times, actors turn to the EU level if they are not supported by decision-makers at the national level. Recent prominent examples have been take-over or merger cases, or when German private banks accused their government of protecting its public sector banks (*Landesbanken*). Thereby the EU has slipped into a multi-layer governance system.

10.1 Conditions and specificities at the EU level

In principle lobbying in the EU or, as it is increasingly called, advocacy or public affairs, is no different than in any national context. Even so,

---

[97] See for instance Bomberg et al. (2008), op. cit. and R. van Schendelen, *More Machiavelli in Brussels*, Amsterdam: Amsterdam University Press, 2010.

there are a number of features related to the EU and the working of its institutions that add a twist to EU lobbying. Instead of a government there is a complex governance structure of interacting institutions at the EU level. In the European Parliament for instance, European-wide parties exist, but compared with the national level they rather resemble associations of national parties from similar political families. Equally there are hardly any European-wide mass media. An organised civil society is only emerging.

Like national institutions, the EU institutions rely on stakeholders and national experts to provide relevant information. The European Commission has put in place a system of consultative committees on a wide range of issues. The current number of these committees is expected to be somewhere around 1,000.[98]

Key factors for the potential influence of a stakeholder are technical expertise (i.e. information) and scope (i.e. legitimacy through representation of a broad range of (pan-European) members). In addition to the provision of information, stakeholders also provide legitimacy for the European institutions. For instance, arguments coming from stakeholders can strengthen the European Commission's position in the decision-making process, with respect to both national governments in the Council and party-political views in the European Parliament. Stakeholder support is thus important for the European Commission to ensure that its policy proposals are making it through the EU's complex decision-making process. Examples of this kind of cooperation include those of the European Commission working with business groups such as the European Round Table of Industrialists to advance the internal market or the European IT Round Table to realise high-tech research programmes like ESPRIT. In some cases the European Commission has undertaken measures to support the participation of interest groups to achieve a more balanced interest representation at the EU level, for example through the organisation of networking events or stakeholder consultations.

---

[98] Based on 2004 figures given by the European Commission following an inquiry by the European Parliament.

A particular challenge for interest representation at the EU level is the complexity and the length of the decision-making process (Figure 8). Rather than having to deal with a central actor (i.e. a government that bases its powers on a solid majority in parliament), powers at the EU level are dispersed among various actors that become important at different stages of the process. As such, the European Commission is the key institution in the initial phase, i.e. when a legislative proposal is prepared. The Council (and in most cases also the European Parliament) are of great importance once the European Commission has presented its proposal, as both institutions are to accept, refuse or (in most instances) amend the proposal. In the implementation phase it is again the European Commission that is the central player at the EU level. The EU adopts roughly 2,500 legal acts per year of which some 20% are legislative acts, mostly undertaken under the ordinary legislative procedure, while 80% are non-legislative acts, such as delegated or implementing acts.

Figure 8. Decision-making pyramid

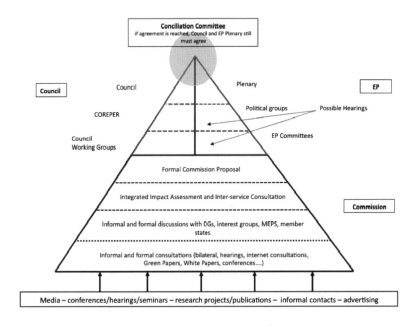

Source: Authors compilation.

The consecutive treaty changes, resulting in the extension of the ordinary legislative procedure, have led to a considerable increase in lobbying activities vis-à-vis the European Parliament during the legislative phase. Interest representatives often focus their activities on the rapporteur. In parallel, lobbies also use their member state base to influence the positions of their national governments in the Council.

10.2 Towards a framework for interest representation at the EU

In response to past accusations that EU institutions tend to work with 'preferred interlocutors', the EU institutions are progressively trying to establish a framework for interest representation. This issue was addressed in the context of the European Commission's White Paper on European Governance from 2001[99] and its follow-up initiatives. A first step has been to rationalise consultation. In 2002, the European Commission unilaterally adopted basic norms for consultation, including inter alia, respect for a minimum period of eight weeks from consultation to decision and the obligation to provide feedback on the outcomes of the consultation. The European Commission is also tasked with consulting with the widest possible variety of stakeholders to ensure a plurality of views, including online consultations. The objective is to create more transparency and more plurality in consultation. In addition, the European Commission is obliged to undertake and publish for any significant legislation an integrated impact assessment to *ex ante* evaluate and quantify – as far as possible – the economic, social or environmental consequences of the proposed legislation. Quite predictably, this has led to a large number of academic studies being conducted in parallel with the European Commission's processes.

With its 2007 follow-up on the European Transparency Initiative,[100] the European Commission decided to gradually establish a

---

[99] See European Commission, European Governance – A White Paper, COM(2001) 428, Brussels, 25 July 2001 (http://ec.europa.eu/governance/white_paper/en.pdf).

[100] See the European Commission's Communication, Follow-up to the Green Paper 'European Transparency Initiative', COM(2007) 127, Brussels, 21 March 2007 (http://ec.europa.eu/civil_society/docs/com_2007_127_final_en.pdf).

framework for the institutions' relations with interest groups. Since 2008, the European Commission has put in place a voluntary register and elaborated a code of conduct for interest groups. The main elements are the disclosure of their identity and their clients' identities (i.e. their interests or those of their clients), objective information on the organisations and a declaration that they will not obtain information in any illegal way. In return, the European Commission has committed to provide information on important meetings and to consult with the registered interest groups. Violation of the code of conduct will result in exclusion from the registry. By mid-summer 2010, around 3,000 organisations were registered, of which more than half were private interest organisations, followed by NGOs and research groups (30%), consultants and law firms. Meanwhile, the European Parliament – which has had its own registry in place since 1999 – has pleaded for a joint European Commission/Parliament registry and a joint working group is currently exploring ways to establish such a registry by mid-2011.

In conclusion, while the EU framework for interest representation is far younger, less developed and entails fewer constraints than for example that of the US, it constitutes a step forward in the governance of lobbying and transparency compared with almost all member states. In particular the registers for expert groups and for interest representatives provide a fair degree of transparency. And what is valid for the EU as a whole is also true for interest representation: it will continue to evolve.

11. The EU's external action

In the past, it has often been said that the EU is a giant when it comes to international trade, but a dwarf in international politics. It has been a long-term challenge of the EU to speak with one voice on international topics, as foreign policy remains one of the emblems of a sovereign nation state. Yet one of the purposes of a Union foreign policy is not to replace states, but to increase the impact that a national foreign policy can have individually, for example in development policy where the EU and member states contribute more than half of the development assistance provided by developed nations. Over the years, the Union has built a complex system of competences and decision-making in foreign affairs. On the one hand, these include exclusive EU competences, like those for trade, where the EU is represented alongside the 27 member states in the World Trade Organisation (WTO). On the other hand, there are shared competences in many areas, such as in neighbourhood policy, development policy, international humanitarian cooperation and in most external dimensions of the internal policies of the Union (e.g. climate, energy, migration, transport, public health and fisheries). In these fields the EU is represented by a combination of the European Commission and member states. The question of the EU's external representation likewise extends to foreign security and defence matters and how the EU is represented in international organisations.

11.1 Common foreign and security policy and the High Representative

Various forms of political cooperation have existed in the EU for many years. The Maastricht Treaty of 1992 established the EU's CFSP as a policy outside the classical Community system with limited powers for the European Commission. The Amsterdam Treaty of 1999 created the position of the High Representative for CFSP (initially held by Javier Solana) mainly to represent the EU externally.

With the Lisbon Treaty, foreign and security policy decisions of the EU are taken by consensus by the Foreign Affairs Council (FAC) or the European Council. Decisions on objectives and strategic pronouncements are typically undertaken by the European Council while the necessary follow-up decisions are guided by the FAC to ensure – together with the High Representative – the "unity, consistency and effectiveness of action by the EU" (Art. 26(2) TEU). Reflecting the organising principle, which is forging "mutual political solidarity" (Art. 24(2) and (3) TEU) among member states, EU foreign and security policy essentially aims at protecting the identified common interests and defending common values. A consequence of this focus is that EU foreign policy-making is largely kept out of the judicial supervision of the European Court of Justice and the political control of the European Parliament, with two exceptions. The European Parliament has budgetary oversight and fully co-decides on the human resources (staff regulations).

In practice, EU foreign and defence policy is based on the following three instruments:

- definition of general guidelines;

- decisions on EU joint actions, propositions and detailed arrangements for implementation; and

- ways to strengthen cooperation systematically among member states.

A crucial innovation is the significant 'beefing-up' of the position of High Representative of the Union for Foreign Affairs and Security policy. The High Representative is the main coordinator and the representative to the outside world. A particular innovation of the Lisbon Treaty is that the High Representative is institutionally anchored in both the Council of Ministers and the European Commission – in the Council as High Representative and in the European Commission as one of its vice presidents, with the portfolio for external relations. The High Representative now also chairs the FAC.

The powers of the High Representative include the right of initiative in foreign policy, alongside (any of) the member states. The High Representative can also put forward a proposal jointly with the European Commission. She chairs the FAC meetings with the exception of the trade discussions, which are chaired by the rotating Council presidency. She also conducts the CFSP and is responsible for the implementation of foreign policy decisions in addition to being responsible for coordination with EU member states in international organisations and at international conferences. The High Representative can address the UN Security Council (UNSC) whenever the Union has a defined position on the issue being discussed and depending on acceptance of the High Representative doing so by the non-EU UNSC members. Added to these responsibilities are those as chairperson of the boards of foreign and security policy-relevant agencies that have been set up to deal with EU-wide capacity building, the development of a common security culture, satellite imagery and education.[101]

---

[101] More specifically these bodies are the European Defence Agency, the EU Institute for Security Studies, the EU Satellite Centre and the European Security and Defence College.

In all those activities, the High Representative is assisted by the European External Action Service (EEAS), which is an EU body of a special nature, having been the result of complex negotiations among the member states, the European Parliament, the European Commission and the High Representative. The service includes civil servants coming from the European Commission, diplomats from the national foreign ministries and officials of the General Secretariat of the Council. At the time of writing the EEAS was in the process of being established. It was officially launched on 1 December 2010 and the process should be fully completed by 2013. Although the head of the EEAS ('appointing authority') is the High Representative, day-to-day business is managed by its Secretary-General, two deputies and a director-general for budget and administration. At the start of its life, the EEAS has fewer than 4,000 staff, compared with about 95,000 diplomats working for the national foreign ministries of the EU-27 member states and over 20,000 for the US State Department (France and Germany have more than 10,000 national diplomats each).

In principle, all decisions on the CFSP are taken by unanimity. Yet sometimes it is possible for a country not to join the others in an action without blocking it. Such an approach is called 'constructive abstention', whereby a country that *abstains* from a CFSP decision is not bound by it, but pledges not to take any unilateral action that might conflict with it. There is also a theoretical possibility of closer cooperation in foreign policy among fewer than 27 member states (enhanced cooperation), but the decision allowing for enhanced cooperation in this policy area needs to be taken by unanimity.

11.2 EU defence cooperation

Contrary to foreign and security policy, defence cooperation among the EU member states is still at an early stage, notwithstanding that defence cooperation began in 1948 with the creation of the Western European Union, the EU's initial defence arm, whose substantive provisions have been submerged into the EU Treaties (see also appendix 1). The current common security and defence policy allows for establishing permanent structured cooperation in defence matters for member states that wish to do so.

The major obstacle for the European countries in advancing this policy has been the national reluctance of member states with respect to developing collective military capabilities. One should keep in mind that the EU comprises four neutral member states (i.e. Austria, Finland, Ireland and Sweden) and a number of additional ones with a very limited military capacity. Nevertheless, the option of embarking on permanent cooperation in defence matters has been created, not least as a tool for introducing flexibility for future integration efforts. The Treaty stipulates that only those member states with military capabilities fulfilling "higher criteria" and having "made more binding commitments to one another" can participate in this defence partnership (Art. 42(6) TEU). Typically for the EU, such selective yet permanent cooperation is to remain open to the initially non-participating states.

The drafting of the so-called 'Petersberg tasks'[102] in 1992 was the first step in that direction. They entailed the establishment of EU battlegroups, which became fully operational in 2007. To date, the EU claims to be able to undertake simultaneously two single, rapid response operations of battlegroup size (about 1,500 soldiers each).

11.3 The EU in international diplomacy and organisations

The Treaty of Lisbon of 2009 has not only reformed decision-making and provided for (some) institutional innovations, it has also addressed representation of the EU in foreign policy, international diplomacy and international organisations. The main innovations are outlined below:

- representation of the EU in international relations is provided by the European Commission on all issues except CFSP;

- representation of the EU in international relations in all CFSP matters is provided by the High Representative, who also oversees coordination among policies;

---

[102] The Petersberg tasks cover humanitarian and rescue tasks, peacekeeping tasks and tasks of combat forces in crisis management, including peacemaking, and as an integral part of the European security and defence policy (ESDP) are included in the Treaty on European Union.

- representation at the highest level of heads of state and government is provided by the President of the European Commission (on all issues except CFSP) and the President of the European Council (on CFSP matters); and

- the EEAS has been set up, with 137 delegations worldwide.

In reality, however, this division of labour can be complex. Moreover, concerning the external representation of the Union, at the time of writing there was still disagreement regarding international negotiations on issues that fall under the shared competence of the Union and member states (so-called 'mixed agreements').

The EU's role in external policies and its representation also depend on non-EU states accepting a uniform EU representation in international fora of which they are part. At one end of the spectrum are international organisations in which the EU has no institutional status, including the UNSC, NATO and the World Bank. Such cases are becoming fewer and fewer, however, and even where they continue to exist, the EU as an actor is gradually being felt.[103]

At the other end of the spectrum are those situations in which the EU has exclusive competences and therefore a preeminent position in the relevant organisations and legal conventions. The major case in point is in the trade policy field, concerning the WTO and the World Customs Organisation. For the WTO in particular the European Commission is the sole negotiator operating under negotiation directives from the member states. In addition to negotiating multilateral trade agreements, this also means that the European Commission negotiates all international bilateral (i.e. EU and third-

---

[103] In the UNSC, the EU is beginning to have some limited access to speak. The EU–NATO relationship is now sometimes described as one of strategic partnership. One could think of fostering this partnership by reciprocal observer status (at the North Atlantic Council and the EU Political and Security Committee). The arrangements at the World Bank represent a major anomaly, since the EU is now a larger aid donor than any of its member states, and its operational partnerships in the European and African regions are important, yet it does not even have observer status on the executive board (only on its ministerial policy committee).

party) agreements. With the Treaty of Lisbon the scope of the EU's trade policy has been extended and now covers trade in goods and services and the commercial aspects of intellectual property as well as foreign direct investment.

The most complex situations arise for the large category of policies that entail shared competences with the EU, where both the EU and member states are present, but where the EU presence spans a broad range from a simple observer alongside many others (e.g. 67 at the UN General Assembly),[104] through 'enhanced observer' or 'virtual member' to full member or contracting party alongside the member states as in a number of important UN conventions and protocols, such as those on ozone depletion, climate change and pesticides, to name but a few. In most cases, both the EU represented by the European Commission and the member states are parties to conventions and protocols. EU representation then depends on legal details in the Treaty and decisions by the EU on how to most efficiently and effectively be represented in the negotiation process.

11.4 Other EU-specific external relations

The framework for development cooperation policy has been largely maintained with the Treaty of Lisbon. If before the EU's policy corresponded with national policies, now the EU's policy and the national ones on development cooperation should "complement and reinforce each other" (Art. 208(1) TFEU). The Union policy is jointly managed by the European Commission (at the operational level) and the European External Action Service (at the strategic level).

The 'neighbourhood policy' portfolio is jointly managed by the High Representative and the respective Commissioner.[105]

---

[104] See M. Emerson et al., *Upgrading the EU's Role as Global Actor*, Centre for European Policy Studies, Egmont – The Royal Institute for International Relations, European Policy Centre and the University of Leuven, Brussels and Leuven, 2011.

[105] The neighbourhood policy covers Belarus, Armenia, Azerbaijan, Ukraine, Moldova and Georgia in Eastern Europe and countries in the southern Mediterranean region, including Jordan.

Neighbourhood policy focuses on states to which the Union offers cooperation much closer than with other partners. With most of such states there are negotiations on a free trade agreement. Several other forms of cooperation take place in specific areas, for instance migration, energy or maritime affairs.

In contrast, EU enlargement policy continues to be managed by the European Commission, but there are geographical desks within the EEAS that also deal with the respective countries on other matters.[106] Enlargement policy aims at preparing the countries concerned to become full EU members when they, as well as the EU, are ready. The conditions for accession are comprehensive and include complete adoption of the EU legal system as well as meeting conditions on democratic governance, the rule of law and respect of human rights.

12.   Conclusion: Understanding the 'ever-changing Union'

More than a year after its entry into force it is certainly still too early for a full assessment of the impact of the Lisbon Treaty on the Union's institutional development. As with any legal text, this Treaty is only a framework that sets the scene for political action to bring it to life and to use its full potential.

Inevitably this short book can only provide a temporary snapshot of an organisation that is subject to constant evolution and change. The Treaty of Lisbon, as the – at least temporary – endpoint of a long process of comprehensive treaty revisions, is set to allow for some consolidation of the Union's basic framework. Future treaty changes are likely to be much more limited in scope and targeted at specific issues (such as the European Stability Mechanism). National leaders will probably also be very hesitant to confer additional competences to the EU in order to avoid referenda.

Irrespective of further treaty amendments, however, there is still large potential for institutional adaptation and change. This partly stems from open questions concerning the concrete implementation and

---

[106] Enlargement policy covers Iceland, the countries of the Western Balkans and Turkey.

institutional practices under the Lisbon Treaty, developments at the sub-treaty level (secondary law, jurisprudence and inter-institutional agreements) and possible initiatives outside the Treaty framework that have a direct impact on it and prospects for future integration (e.g. as happened in the past with the Schengen Agreement).

Owing to the complex structures of the EU, which have never been designed according to a master plan, many Europeans (and non-Europeans) still lack even a basic understanding of how the EU functions. With this guide the authors hope that they have increased general knowledge among readers and stimulated their interest in knowing more about how the EU works.

Glossary of key terms and abbreviations

APS   Annual Policy Strategy, previously the strategic programme for the year ahead, which has since been replaced by the 'state of the union' address by the President of the European Commission before the plenary of the European Parliament.

Bretton Woods System   System of fixed currency exchange rates launched after World War II.

CEECs   Central and Eastern European countries previously under Soviet Union dominance (later joining the EU in 2004).

CFSP   Common foreign and security policy (of the EU)

Co-decision   The EU's principal legislative procedure through which both the Council of Ministers and the European Parliament co-decide on the basis of a Commission proposal (referred to as the →'ordinary legislative procedure' since the →Treaty of Lisbon).

Comitology   This term traditionally referred to the monitoring of the European Commission's executive powers by way of committees chaired by the European Commission and composed of representatives from each member state. With the Treaty of Lisbon, this system has been overhauled and a division between quasi-legislative acts ('delegated acts') and mere implementing acts has been introduced. A revised comitology system applies solely to the latter.

Community method   An expression used for the institutional operating mode marked by a supranational stance (rather than an intergovernmental one) with due respect for the →subsidiarity principle. It has the following salient features:

- the European Commission's monopoly of the right of initiative;
- widespread use of qualified majority voting in the Council;

- the European Parliament and Council of Ministers having the same powers concerning the amendment of legislative proposals from the European Commission; and

- a uniform interpretation of Community law by the European Court of Justice.

Consent procedure	The consent procedure is one of the 'special legislative procedures' of the Treaty of Lisbon. Under this procedure, adoption of a legislative act only requires the consent of the European Parliament, which cannot suggest concrete amendments, as is the case under the →ordinary legislative procedure.
Constitutional Treaty	This Treaty was prepared by the Convention on the Future of Europe and the subsequent →Intergovernmental Conference; it ultimately failed to secure ratification in France and the Netherlands, but many elements were later taken up in the →Treaty of Lisbon.
Consultation procedure	The consultation procedure is one of the 'special legislative procedures' of the Treaty of Lisbon. Under this procedure, adoption of a legislative act only requires consultation of the European Parliament.
CoR	The Committee of the Regions is an advisory body composed of representatives of regional and local authorities in EU member states; it was established by the Treaty of Maastricht.
COREPER	French acronym for the Committee of Permanent Representatives, composed of EU member states' ambassadors or deputy ambassadors (respectively COREPER II or I) who deal with draft laws before they are passed to ministers in the →Council of Ministers.
COSI	Standing Committee on Internal Security, introduced by the →Treaty of Lisbon to promote and strengthen cooperation on internal security within the EU (Art. 71 TFEU).

Council of Ministers	The Council of Ministers (also referred to as the 'Council') groups member states at ministerial level to normally co-decide with the European Parliament on EU law. The Council currently meets in 10 different formations, depending on the policy issue; there are some 100 Council meetings annually.
Court of Auditors	EU institution to audit EU financial management.
DG	Directorate-General, normally a department within the European Commission. DG is also the term used in other EU institutions.
EBA	European Banking Authority
EC	European Community, a founding element of the European integration process. It was established as the →EEC (European Economic Community) by the Treaty of Rome in 1957, with the principal objective of creating a common market without internal borders. The establishment of the European Union in 1992 did not cause the European Economic Community to disappear. It remained part of the EU under the designation 'European Community'; sometimes EC is also (confusingly) used as an abbreviation for the →European Commission.
EC 1992	Programme to complete the →EC internal market following the →Single European Act (SEA).
ECB	European Central Bank, created by the →Treaty of Maastricht and independent of the EU member states; headquarters in Frankfurt.
ECHR	European Convention on Human Rights; with the Treaty of Lisbon the EU is obliged to accede to the ECHR (accession negotiations are underway at the time of writing); all EU member states are parties to the Convention.
Ecofin	A Council of Ministers formation dealing with economic and financial affairs; Ecofin is one of the most important Council configurations.
ECSC	European Coal and Steel Community, created by the first of the 'European' Treaties in 1952.
EDF	European Development Fund

EEA	European Economic Area, formed through a cooperation agreement between the EU and Norway, Iceland and Liechtenstein, and enabling the latter countries to take part in the EU's internal market and some other policies.
EEC	European Economic Community, established by the →Treaty of Rome in 1957, with the principal objective of creating a common market without internal borders (→EC).
EESC	European Economic and Social Committee; a consultative body of the EU composed of employers' organisations, trade unions and representatives of various other interests. It is similar to the →Committee of the Regions (CoR).
EFSF	European Financial Stability Facility; established as a Luxembourg-registered company by the member states of the euro area in 2010 for a limited period (three years). From 2013 onwards it shall be replaced by a permanent stability mechanism (→ESM), which requires a treaty change (i.e. ratification by all EU member states), however. As part of an overall rescue package of €750 billion, the EFSF is able to issue bonds guaranteed by the euro countries for up to €440 billion for on-lending to euro countries in difficulty, subject to conditions negotiated with the European Commission in liaison with the European Central Bank and International Monetary Fund and to be approved by the Eurogroup.
EFSM	European Financial Stabilisation Mechanism; also a part of the overall rescue package (like the →EFSF) with €60 billion guaranteed by the EU budget. The mechanism is managed by the European Commission and based on Art. 122(2) TFEU and on an intergovernmental agreement among euro countries.
EIOPA	European Insurance and Occupational Pensions Authority.
EMS	European monetary system, precursor to the →EMU.

EMU	Economic and Monetary Union
Enhanced cooperation	Allows those countries of the Union that wish to continue to work more closely together to do so, while respecting the single institutional framework of the Union as laid out in the Treaties.
EPSO	European Personnel Selection Office, which manages the recruitment of EU officials and contractual agents.
ERC	European Research Council; European funding body to support 'frontier research'.
ESM	European Stability Mechanism; permanent mechanism to succeed the temporary →EFSF after 2013; it will require amendment of the →TFEU (i.e. ratification by all member states).
ESMA	European Securities and Markets Authority
Euratom	Atomic Energy Community, founded in 1957, as part of the →Treaties of Rome.
Eurogroup	Meeting of the finance ministers of eurozone countries.
Eurojust	Eurojust is the EU's judicial cooperation body created to improve the fight against serious crime by facilitating coordination of action for investigations and prosecutions covering the territory of more than one member state. Eurojust is composed of 27 members from each member state (senior judges, prosecutors or police officers).
Europe à la carte	An unofficial term referring to a non-uniform concept of integration that would allow member states to selectively participate in policies.
European Citizens' Initiative	A million EU citizens will be able to ask (but not force) the European Commission to present new policy initiatives that fall within its area of competence.
European Commission	This EU institution is responsible for implementing and managing EU policies (except →CFSP), legislative proposals and respect of EU law (in its role as 'guardian of the Treaties').

European Council	The meeting of the heads of state and government in the EU to provide strategic direction; since the →Treaty of Lisbon, it has become an EU institution with a full-time elected President.
European Court of Justice (ECJ)	EU supreme judiciary in most policy areas except foreign (→CFSP), security and defence policies.
European Defence Community	This attempt in the early 1950s to integrate the armies of the original six members was later aborted.
European External Action Service (EEAS)	EU 'diplomatic corps' set up by the →Treaty of Lisbon.
European Parliament (EP)	The European Parliament consists of directly elected →MEPs.
Europol	European Police Office, the European law enforcement agency dealing with cross-border matters.
European Political Union (EPU)	This attempt (in 1952–53) to create an integrated European foreign policy was later aborted.
Eurosclerosis	An unofficial term describing a period in the 1970s and early 1980s marked by a perceived stagnation of European integration, partly owing to high unemployment and slow job creation in spite of overall economic growth.
FAC	Foreign Affairs Council, a meeting of EU foreign affairs ministers that is part of the →Council of Ministers.
G-7	Periodic meeting of the world's leading industrialised countries to cooperate on international economic and monetary issues. It was formed in 1976, when Canada joined the Group of Six: France, Germany, Italy, Japan, the UK and US.
G-8	By adding Russia, the G-7 became the G-8. The EU is represented within the G-8, but cannot host or chair it.
G-20	The G-20 consists of the members of the G-7 plus 12 other nations (including China, India, Brazil, Saudi Arabia and Russia) and the EU (which cannot host or chair it). The G-20 was formed in 1999 as a forum for member nations to discuss key issues related to the global economy.

GAC	General Affairs Council, the meeting of EU foreign ministers or state secretaries for EU affairs of the member states; it forms part of the →Council of Ministers and meets monthly.
High Authority	This supranational administrative executive of the European Coal and Steel Community (→ECSC) first took office in 1952 in Luxembourg, and later became the →European Commission.
High Representative	High Representative for the common foreign and security policy (→CFSP), created under the →Treaty of Amsterdam to coordinate and externally represent the EU's CFSP.
IGC	An Intergovernmental Conference gathers together representatives of member states' governments with a view to amending the EU Treaties.
JHA	Justice and home affairs in the EU context involves cooperation on matters of internal security, immigration and judicial matters (→PJCC, →pillar structure).
MEP	Member of the →European Parliament
NATO	North Atlantic Treaty Organisation, the principal Western and therefore European security and defence framework founded after World War II.
OECD	Organisation for Economic Cooperation and Development
Ordinary legislative procedure	Name of the EU's principal legislative procedure following the →Treaty of Lisbon, whereby both the Council of Ministers and the European Parliament decide on a final text through →co-decision.
Pillar structure	Between 1993 and 2009, the EU legally consisted of three pillars, which was abandoned with the entry into force of the →Treaty of Lisbon, when the EU acquired a single legal personality. The three pillars consisted of 1) a European Community pillar, which covered economic, social and environmental policies; 2) the common foreign and security policy (→CFSP), which covered foreign policy and military matters; and

	3) police and judicial cooperation in criminal matters (→PJCC), which brought together cooperation in the fight against crime. This pillar originally incorporated all matters pertaining to →justice and home affairs (JHA), but the →Treaty of Amsterdam moved large parts of JHA policies to the Community pillar.
PJCC	Police and judicial cooperation in criminal matters, which under the Amsterdam and Nice Treaties made up the third EU →pillar (under the earlier Maastricht Treaty, this pillar had been referred to as cooperation on →justice and home affairs (JHA)).
PSC	The Political and Security Committee (also referred to by its French acronym, COPS) is a permanent body in the field of common foreign and security policy mentioned in Art. 25 of the Treaty on European Union (→TEU).
QMV	Qualified majority voting, whereby a qualified majority of the number of votes is required in the Council of Ministers for a decision to be adopted when issues are not decided under the unanimity rule.
Schengen	The Schengen Agreement was signed on 14 June 1985 by some member states to remove controls at their common borders and introduce freedom of movement for all nationals of the signatory member states, other member states or non-EU countries.
	Originally outside the framework of the EU Treaties, since 1999 it has formed part of the institutional and legal framework of the EU by virtue of a protocol to the →Treaty of Amsterdam.
	The Schengen Agreement has been extended over time to all member states except Ireland and the UK, Bulgaria, Romania and Cyprus. Non-EU countries Iceland, Norway and Switzerland are also members.
Schuman Plan	The Schuman Plan, which led to the Schuman Declaration on 9 May 1950, was a proposal by then French foreign minister Robert Schuman to create a new form of organisation of states in Europe, calling

	for a supranational Community; seen as the origin of the EU (→ECSC, EEC, Euratom, EC).
SEA	Single European Act; reform of the EU Treaties as a reaction to the period of →Eurosclerosis. The SEA entered into force in 1987 and led to the creation of the internal market (→EC 1992).
Second pillar	Common foreign and security policy (→CFSP) pillar covering foreign policy and military matters prior to the →Treaty of Lisbon (see also →pillar structure).
Stability and Growth Pact (SGP)	The SGP aims at ensuring that member states maintain budgetary discipline after adopting the single currency.
Subsidiarity principle	The principle of subsidiarity stipulates that the EU should only act in those areas where the same result cannot be achieved just as well at the national (regional or local) levels.
TEC	Treaty establishing the European Community; renamed →TFEU by the →Treaty of Lisbon.
TEU	Treaty on European Union (also referred to as the →Treaty of Maastricht); the TEU introduced the EU's →pillar structure, which was later formally abandoned by the →Treaty of Lisbon.
TFEU	Treaty on the Functioning of the European Union; formerly the Treaty on European Community (→TEC), which was subsequently amended and renamed TFEU by the →Treaty of Lisbon.
Third pillar	The pillar on police and judicial cooperation in criminal matters (→PJCC) brought together cooperation in the fight against crime prior to the →Treaty of Lisbon (see also →pillar structure). This pillar was originally much broader and encompassed all matters pertaining to →justice and home affairs (JHA).
Treaty of Amsterdam	Reform treaty that entered into force in 1999; it amended the →TEU and →TEC.
Treaty of Lisbon	Reform treaty that entered into force in 2009; it amended the →TEU and →TEC (renaming the latter the →TFEU).

Treaty of Maastricht	Reform treaty that entered into force in 1993; it amended the Treaty establishing the European Economic Community (TEEC), renaming the latter the →TEC. The Treaty of Maastricht is also referred to as the→TEU.
Treaty of Nice	Reform treaty that entered into force in 2003; it amended the →TEU and →TEC.
Treaty(ies) of Rome	Two treaties that entered into force on 1 January 1958 at the origin of European integration, namely the →EEC and →Euratom Treaties.

For further information, see the website of the European Commission, "Europa Glossary" (http://europa.eu/scadplus/glossary/index_en.htm).

References

Bomberg, E., J. Peterson and A. Stubb (2008), *The European Union: How Does it Work?*, Oxford: Oxford University Press.

Cockfield, A. (1994), *The European Union: Creating the Single Market*, Chichester: John Wiley and Sons.

Dinan, D. (2010), *Ever Closer Union: An Introduction to European Integration*, 4th edition, London: Palgrave Macmillan.

Emerson, M., R. Balfour, T. Corthaut, J. Wouters, P.M. Kaczyński and T. Renard (2011), *Upgrading the EU's Role as Global Actor*, Centre for European Policy Studies, Egmont – The Royal Institute for International Relations, European Policy Centre and the University of Leuven, Brussels and Leuven.

Hagemann, S. and J. De Clerck-Sachsse (2007), *Old Rules, New Game: Decision-making in the Council of Ministers after the 2004 Enlargement*, CEPS Special Report, Centre for European Policy Studies, Brussels, March.

Hix, S. (2008), *What's wrong with the European Union and how to fix it*, 1st edition, Cambridge, UK and Malden, MA: Polity Press.

Kaczyński, P.M., P. ó Broin, F. Dehousse, P. de Schoutheete, T. Heremans, J. Keller, G. Milton, N. Witney, J. Emmanouilidis, A. Missiroli and C. Stratulat (2010), *The Treaty of Lisbon: A Second Look at the Institutional Innovations*, Joint study by Centre for European Policy Studies, Egmont and European Policy Centre, Brussels.

Kauppi, H. and W. Widgrén (2006), *Voting rules and budget allocation in an enlarged EU*, CEPR Discussion Paper No. 5134, Centre for Economic and Policy Research, London.

Kiljunen, K. (2004), *The European Constitution in the Making*, Centre for European Policy Studies, Brussels.

Kurpas, S., C. Grøn and P.M. Kaczyński (2008), *The European Commission after enlargement: Does more add up to less?*, CEPS Special Report, Centre for European Policy Studies, Brussels, February.

Ludlow, P. (2004), *The Making of the New Europe*, EuroComment, Brussels.

Norman, P. (2005), *The Accidental Constitution*, 2nd edition, EuroComment, Brussels.

Nugent, N. (2010), *The Government and Politics of the European Union*, 7th edition, London: Palgrave Macmillan.

Pelkmans, J. (2006), *European Integration – Methods and Economic Analysis*, 3rd edition, Pearson Education.

Piris, J.-C. (2010), *The Lisbon Treaty: A Legal and Political Analysis*, Cambridge: Cambridge University Press.

Van Schaik, L., M. Kaeding, A. Hudson and J. Núñez Ferrer (eds) (2006), *Policy Coherence for Development in the Council: Strategies for the way forward*, Centre for European Policy Studies, Brussels.

Van Schendelen, R. (2010), *More Machiavelli in Brussels*, Amsterdam: Amsterdam University Press.

Wallace, H., W. Wallace and M.A. Pollack (2005), *Policy-Making in the European Union*, 5th edition, Oxford: Oxford University Press.

Wiener, A. and T. Diez (2009), *European Integration Theory*, 2nd edition, Oxford: Oxford University Press.

Appendix 1. Post-War European Organisations

In addition to the EU, a great number of organisations have been created to deal with the architecture of Europe after the Second World War, the most important of which are described below.

Council of Europe

The Council of Europe (started in 1949) is a forum for political discussion in which 47 European countries, including all EU countries, Turkey and Russia, meet to discuss political issues. Its main political significance pertains to cultural and human rights issues, notably through its court, the European Court of Human Rights based in Strasbourg. According to the Treaty of Lisbon, the EU is foreseen to accede to the European Convention for the Protection of Human Rights and Fundamental Freedoms (ECHR). Accession negotiations began on 7 July 2010.

Defence and security organisations

Western European Union. The WEU was founded in 1948 (Brussels Treaty) as a defence pool among Western European countries. It included the Netherlands, Belgium, Luxembourg, France and the UK; Germany and Italy joined later. With the decision to create an integrated military structure within NATO in 1951, the WEU lost its appeal. In the early 1990s there were attempts to revive the organisation and to use it as a security and defence profile for the EU. The Amsterdam Treaty integrated the WEU into the EU. On 31 March 2010, the contracting parties decided to terminate the Treaty because the "WEU has...accomplished its historical role"[107] and close down the organisation in 2011.

---

[107] According to the contracting parties, Belgium, France, Germany, Greece, Italy, Luxembourg, the Netherlands, Portugal, Spain and the UK, the WEU has made its "contribution to peace and stability in Europe and to the development of the European security and defence architecture, promoting consultations and cooperation in this field, and conducting operations in a number of theatres, including [the] Petersberg tasks".

North Atlantic Treaty Organisation (NATO). Founded in 1949, NATO was and still is the main basis for collective Western defence and security. The decision to create an integrated military structure fostered NATO's role as the anchor for Western European security. From the mid-1980s, various attempts have been made to strengthen the European pillar of the North Atlantic alliance. With the end of the cold war, NATO has also been redefining its role in a changed political and economic environment. On several occasions NATO has admitted new members from Eastern Europe. To avoid being seen as a threat by Russia, NATO has developed a partnership with Russia. Turkey has been a member of NATO since 1952.

Organisation for Security and Cooperation in Europe (OSCE). OSCE is a body through which East and West meet to discuss security, human rights and cooperation issues. At one time it was expected to develop into a crucial organisation in the pan-European security architecture. The end of the cold war ended this ambition, however. Today the OSCE has nevertheless become a body through which Europe, Russia and Central Asia discuss emerging security questions.

Economic organisations

United Nations Economic Commission for Europe (UNECE). The emergency organisations of the United Nations and European governments were combined in the UNECE in 1946. During the cold war it had some success in bringing about pan-European cooperation in research, highway mapping, statistics and the removal of some obstacles to East–West trade. Although traditionally a bridge between East and West, the UNECE's significance has diminished rather than increased. Its current importance for East–West relations is eclipsed by the EU, the International Monetary Fund, the European Bank for Reconstruction and Development and the Organisation for Economic Cooperation and Development.

Organisation for Economic Cooperation and Development (OECD). The OECD was originally set up to restore free trade and foster closer European economic cooperation. Its first success was the creation of the European Payments Union (set up in 1950). It also successfully pursued a programme to remove trade quotas. Currently the OECD has a membership that includes all industrialised countries (the EU countries, the US, Japan, Canada, etc.) and concentrates on broader international issues of economic cooperation and development. The OECD's main role is to provide authoritative economic analysis, statistics and policy advice in a host of fields. Closely related organisations are the International Transport Forum for coordination in the field of transport and the International Energy Agency, to support the interests of energy-importing countries – originally founded to counter OPEC.

European Free Trade Association (EFTA). The EFTA was formed as a free trade area in response to the formation of a customs union by the then six member states of the European Economic Community. The scope of EFTA did not go beyond industrial and some processed agricultural goods. For some time EFTA's future has been uncertain with Austria, Finland and Sweden having later become EU members. The current members of EFTA are Switzerland, Norway, Iceland and Liechtenstein. On 16 July 2009 Iceland applied to join the EU, with accession negotiations having started on 27 July 2010.

European Economic Area (EEA). The EEA is composed of the EU, Norway, Iceland and Liechtenstein. Economically, the three EEA countries are in fact fully integrated into the EU, as they fall under the single market rules and EU laws on competition and free movement. (The only exceptions in the economic field are thus the common agricultural and fisheries policies of the EU.) In addition, EEA members are equal to full EU members in a number of funding programmes, such as research funding, and they pay into the EU budget. They only have limited means to influence economic regulation (e.g. single market legislation), however, as they do not have a seat on the Council of Ministers. A Joint Committee consisting of the EEA countries and the European Commission has the function of extending relevant EU law to the EEA countries.

Appendix 2. The Ordinary Legislative Procedure

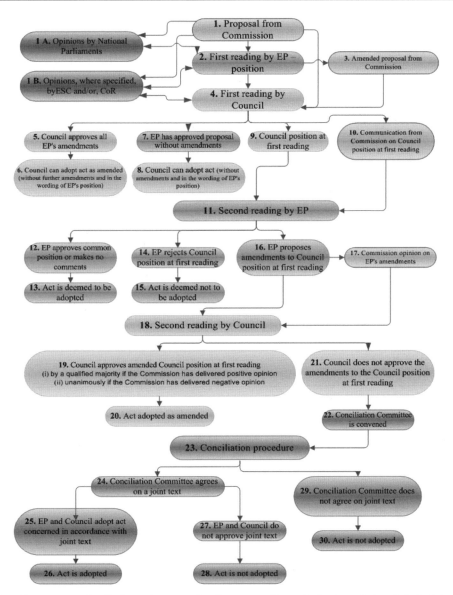

Note: For a more detailed version, see the European Commission's website, "Codecision", Brussels, 30 July 2010 (http://ec.europa.eu/codecision/stepbystep/text/index_en.htm).

Source: European Commission (http://ec.europa.eu/codecision/images/codecision-flowchart_en.gif).

About the Authors

Christian Egenhofer is a Senior Research Fellow at the Centre for European Policy Studies (CEPS), Brussels and a Visiting Professor at the College of Europe (Natolin and Bruges), Sciences Po (Paris) and the LUISS University in Rome (e-mail: christian.egenhofer@ceps.eu).

Sebastian Kurpas is an official at the Secretariat-General of the European Commission. Previously, he was Head of the Politics and Institutions section and a Research Fellow at the Centre for European Policy Studies (CEPS), Brussels (e-mail: sebastian.kurpas@web.de).

Piotr Maciej Kaczyński is a Research Fellow at the Centre for European Policy Studies (CEPS), Brussels. Earlier he served as Head of the European Programme at the Institute of Public Affairs (IPA) in Warsaw (e-mail: piotr.kaczynski@ceps.eu).

Louise van Schaik is a Research Fellow at the Netherlands Institute of International Relations Clingendael and an Associate Research Fellow at the Centre for European Policy Studies (CEPS), Brussels (e-mail: lschaik@clingendael.nl).